Folklore of
OXFORDSHIRE

Folklore of OXFORDSHIRE

Christine Bloxham

TEMPUS

Frontispiece: The King's Men, part of the monument known as the Rollright Stones

First published 2005

Tempus Publishing Limited
The Mill, Brimscombe Port,
Stroud, Gloucestershire, GL5 2QG
www.tempus-publishing.com

British Library Cataloguing in Publication Data.
A catalogue record for this book is available from the British Library.

ISBN 0 7524 3664 3

Typesetting and origination by Tempus Publishing Limited
Printed in Great Britain

CONTENTS

	Acknowledgements	6
	Introduction	7
one	Folklore of Archaeological Sites	8
two	Historical Legends	23
three	Church Lore	50
four	Rites of Passage	54
five	The World of Work	67
six	Hearth and Home	78
seven	Sports and Games	84
eight	The Natural World	92
nine	Seasonal Customs	104
ten	Morris Dancing and Mummers' Plays	125
eleven	The Supernatural	139
twelve	Local Rhymes	154
thirteen	University Customs	167
	Bibliography	180
	Index	185

ACKNOWLEDGEMENTS

My greatest debt of gratitude is owed to David Watts, who has generously allowed me access to his wonderful photographic collection, taken several photographs especially for this book, checked the text for me and given me moral support. His photographs are on pages: 2, 8, 9, 10, 12, 14, 18, 21, 24, 25, 28, 30, 31, 32, 36, 37, 38, 39, 40, 41, 42, 44, 47, 48, 50, 51, 55, 60, 69, 71, 75, 76, 78, 85, 89, 92, 112, 118, 143, 147, 149, 150, 151, 152, 166, 168, and 169.

I am also extremely grateful to the following people who have let me use photographs: Abingdon Traditional Morris Men for photographs on pages 127, 128 and 129 on morris dancing; All Souls College for page 171, the Mallard medal; Bampton Museum for nos 67, 72 and 79 on morris dancing and mummers; Nick Capon for page 98, the Swan Upping; Banbury Museum for page 161, the lady on a white horse and page 162, the Banbury Puritan, which were photographed by Jon Hall; Ray Barrett for page 132, Eynsham Morris Men; Headington Quarry Morris Men for pages 59 and 134, a triumphal marriage arch and mummers; Freda Kitcher for page 69 top, 118 bottom and 119, the Burford Dragon; Oxford Stamp Centre for photographs on pages 109, 110 and 111 on May Day; Oxfordshire County Council Centre for Oxfordshire Studies for page 131, the Headington Morris Men; Paul B. Minet for page 16, the scouring of the White horse and page 86 from his 1972 reprint of *The Scouring of the White Horse* by Thomas Hughes; The Pitt Rivers Museum, University of Oxford for the peeling horn photograph on page 116; *Top Oxon* for the drawing of Somerton maze on page 20; illustrations on pages 25, 30, 36 and 168 are from *The Oxford Pageant*, 1907.

I am grateful to Elizabeth Swaffield for the quotation from Flora Thompson's *Lark Rise to Candleford,* to Mike Balsan for permission to quote from *On the Press* (Boyd 2003) and to Pollinger Ltd and the estate of Mollie Harris for a quotation from *The Green Years.* I would also like to thank David Carpen, Ruth Power and Barbara Reast.

I have made every attempt to contact copyright holders and apologise to any I have been unable to trace.

I have drawn extensively on the work of Percy Manning, the first collector of Oxfordshire folklore, which is now in the Bodleian Library, and of that of Christina Hole, Miss Stanley Smith, Oxford and District Folklore Society and Keith Chandler on morris dancing.

I am also grateful to my editor Matilda Pearce, my husband Norman Blanks and sons Richard and Peter for their patience as I have neglected household duties in favour of writing.

INTRODUCTION

Oxfordshire has a rich heritage, which is reflected in the diversity of its customs and folklore. These reflect the differing aspects such as the lore relating to its wonderful archaeological heritage including the Rollright Stones and Wayland's Smithy, the forest lore of Wychwood, with its poaching and high-waymen and strong tradition of morris dancing, and the close-knit wetland of Otmoor, where men stood together to resist drainage. Its importance in the Civil War is reflected in historical legends and ghost stories. Banbury, the second largest town, is famous for the lady on a white horse rhyme. Oxford boasts the oldest university in Britain, which has its own character and customs. The Vale of White Horse only became part of Oxfordshire in 1974, but has already become part of the rich tapestry of the county.

Some people see customs and folklore as quaint survivals, but they illustrate many changes in beliefs and practices over the centuries, showing another aspect of social history, and give the ordinary people who are often neglected by history a voice.

It is beyond the scope of this book to give a complete picture of the county's customs and folklore, but it aims to provide an introduction and there is a list of sources to encourage further investigation. A more comprehensive look at Oxfordshire's seasonal customs, morris dancing and mummers can be found in my book *May Day to Mummers*.

one

FOLKLORE OF
ARCHAEOLOGICAL SITES

The Rollright Stones

Traces can still be seen of Oxfordshire's ancient landscape, developed over millennia, which later generations have attempted to explain by making up stories about them. The only stone circle to survive locally is the Rollright Stones, situated on a scarp slope north of Chipping Norton, which has more folklore attached to it than any other site in England. It is very difficult to date such sites precisely, but the small group of stones in a field adjoining the circle, known as the Whispering Knights, is the remains of a Neolithic long barrow, erected around 3800-3000 BC, the circle of stones (the King's Men) from between 2500-2000 BC, the late Neolithic, and the single King Stone standing on the horizon, probably a marker for a Bronze Age barrow, from around 1800-1500 BC. Stone circles look immutable, but it seems likely, from recent archaeological fieldwork undertaken by George Lambrick, that the circle has changed considerably, having originally been a large circle of approximately 105 stones closely packed to make a continuous wall with a narrow entrance at the south-south-east. Some stones have been removed, others are broken, and about a third of them were repositioned around 1882.

Engraving of the Rollright Stones with the King Stone, (marked with an 'A'). There is a legend that the petrified king and his soldiers sleep in a cave beneath the stones and will wake and aid England when required. (From Stukeley's *Abury – a Temple of the British Druids with some others, Described*)

Despite these changes, the site has a real aura of mystery today. The principal legend is of its origin: a certain king was on his way to battle when he met a witch, sometimes known as Mother Shipton, from Shipton-under-Wychwood (who may have lived from 1488-1551, and was first mentioned in 1641). The king asked the witch to foretell his future in battle. She responded:

> Seven long strides shalt thou take, and
> If Long Compton thou canst see,
> King of England shalt thou be.

The king was jubilant as the top of the hill was not far away and he was confident he would see Long Compton in the next valley. However as he neared the top a long barrow rose up in front of him, obscuring his view, and the witch cackled with glee:

> As Long Compton thou canst not see,
> King of England thou shalt not be.
> Rise up stick, and stand still, stone,
> For King of England thou shalt be none,
> Thou and thy men hoar stones shall be,
> And I myself an eldern tree.

She then turned the king into stone, his army into the circle and a group of soldiers plotting against him into the Whispering Knights. Another version has a Danish General:

> Said the Danish General
> If Long Compton I cou'd see
> Then King of England I shou'd be.
> But reply'd the British General,
> Then rise up Hill and stand fast Stone –
> For King of England thou'lt be none.

It is said that the stones can never be counted. Certainly this is difficult today as there are broken fragments. A Victorian baker who was determined to count them accurately brought a basket containing a pre-counted number of loaves, and put one down on each stone, but either he had not included enough loaves or they mysteriously vanished and he failed in his quest. Another version says that if anyone can count the same number three times in succession he can have any wish come true. Some believed the stones would join hands and dance in the air at midnight, and go to drink at midnight on New Year's Eve, or when they heard Long Compton clock strike midnight. Sick people have stood in the centre of the stones to pray for recovery.

The witch was said to have changed herself into an elder tree. A festival of cakes and ale was held on Midsummer Eve, when the elder is in bloom. People stood in a circle round the tree, and as they ritually cut it the red sap resembled blood and the King Stone was thought to move his head. Bleeding a witch was supposed to remove her magic powers. Long Compton was rife with witchcraft in the nineteenth century and as late as 1955 a witch's split-ended hazel wand was

Left: The King Stone has changed shape over the years, as drovers carved chips from it 'to keep the Devil off', so too did soldiers as recently as the First World War for good luck. Childless women touched the King Stone with bare breasts to encourage fertility.

Below: People hoped to discover their fortune by listening to the sounds emanating from the Whispering Knights. Twenty horses dragged one stone away to bridge a stream, but two men were killed in the process. It would not stay in place and was said to turn itself over each night, so it was dragged back by a single horse. Another stone was used to dam a millpond, but the water drained out of the pond each night.

discovered at the stones, which was presented to the Museum of Witchcraft at Boscastle in Cornwall.

There is more to the stones than meets the eye: Project Merlin, undertaken in 1979-80, discovered ultrasonic pulsing around the stones which varied in intensity at different times of the year and in different seasons, and was sometimes stronger around the King Stone and sometimes from the circle. The power from the stones sometimes feels welcoming and is sometimes able to repel a person away, and when a dowser, Enid Smithett, began to feel faint and dropped her pendulum in the long grass, instead of flopping on the ground it stood rigidly.

The Devil's Quoits

Another stone circle, the Devil's Quoits, stood at Stanton Harcourt until the Second World War. Local legend says that officers hid behind the stones from bullets, some of which became embedded in the stones. It was said to have been created when the Devil was playing quoits on a Sunday, on being told that he was breaking Sunday observance regulations, he hurled them in fury and they formed the circle. Again, a stone was removed to make a bridge, but it was ill-omened and soon the stone was returned. One legend says that there was fighting in the area, and that the general, Harcourt, was buried in the churchyard. This story arose because for many years the Harcourt family lived at Stanton Harcourt.

Three stones from the Devil's Quoits at Stanton Harcourt, destroyed during the Second World War to build an airfield. (Photograph by Henry Taunt for *Blenheim, Woodstock etc.: Their Story and Some of the Scenes Around Them*)

Standing Stones and Barrows

There are several single standing stones in Oxfordshire. The Hoar Stone near Enstone crossroads is the remains of a Neolithic chamber tomb. Some say that it was erected in memory of a General Hoar, who was killed during the Civil War. Others say it is a 'War Stone' marking the site of a battle, or even that it was set up at a French wedding! It is sometimes known as 'Old Soldier'. It is said to go to drink at midnight on Midsummer Eve, or when it hears the Lidstone church clock strike midnight (although it has no clock) and if moved will return to its original site of its own accord. However, the stones did not like to be seen moving and if anyone was unfortunate enough to do so, the stones would chase and crush them. Some say that it resembles a man mounted on horseback, and is the remains of a Ditchley squire who was out riding with his dog when he was unfortunate enough to be petrified by a witch.

The monolith at Lyneham near Shipton-under-Wychwood is said to drink from the River Evenlode when Shipton church strikes midnight. Allegedly some people returning late from Chipping Norton met it on its way back to the field. The Hoar Stone at Barton Park, near Hopcroft's Holt, is a small group of stones, again the remains of a long barrow. Anyone who moved a stone would be unable to sleep until it was returned. Someone apparently tried to disprove the legend and moved a stone, but could get no sleep at all for three nights and rapidly returned it. Some farmers believed that the stones had grown from 'little uns', others that if they were moved they would return home of their own accord.

The Hawk Stone near Spelsbury is said to go to drink when it hears the clock strike twelve. The large slit in the top is said to have been made when witches were chained to it and burned. (Photograph by Henry Taunt for *Blenheim, Woodstock etc.: Their Story and Some of the Scenes Around Them*)

The Thor stone at Taston was thought to exert an evil influence, so much so that the Cross was used to avert its power. A large stone was said to have been thrown by the Devil from Beacon Hill at Chinnor church, but failed to reach its mark.

Joseph's or Jacob's Stone, which stands at an intersection of trackways near the centre of Otmoor, has been described as a Roman milestone, an old surveyors' mark or a mounting block. A drawing of 1817 in the Bodleian Library shows it as a mounting block with an inscription:

> Joseph Guilder brought this stone
> To help people up when they were down.

Another version of the inscription went:

> Joseph's stone of high renown
> To help me up when I am down
> On my way to the seven towns.

The 'seven towns' refers to the villages of Otmoor. Beckley residents described the stone as 'half a round stone' which rotated once every twenty-four hours.

Legends have grown up around Neolithic and Bronze Age barrows, which have sometimes been reused by the Romans and Anglo-Saxons. At Garsington the place names Dragonhoard and Brokenbarrow, found as early as the thirteenth century, suggest a hoard of treasure in a barrow guarded by a dragon. A round barrow at Cuckhamsley, East Hendred, allegedly the site of a pre-Norman gemot or public meeting place, is said to be the tomb of a Captain Scutchamer who was killed during the Civil War. Attempts to excavate it have been frustrated by thunderstorms.

Circles visible in the ground in dry seasons at Brighthampton near Standlake, which indicate traces of barrows, or Iron Age huts or ditches, were thought by the locals to be the site of fairy rings.

Wayland's Smithy

The most famous Neolithic long barrow in Oxfordshire is Wayland's Smithy, situated by the Ridgeway in the Vale of White Horse. It was constructed in two phases, the first holding the remains of about fourteen bodies. The second phase with three burial chambers constructed of sarsen stones contains eight burials. It was a significant site in the Neolithic era, and its importance has since been maintained in local folklore. It has been known as Wayland's Smithy since Anglo-Saxon times, being named as such in a charter of AD 955. Wayland, or Weyland, was described as a giant in Anglo-Saxon mythology, the son of a heroic sailor, Wade, and a mermaid, famed for his skills as a smith and maker of legendary armour and swords. He married a Valkyrie, but she left him to return to her own world. Wayland was captured by the King of Sweden and imprisoned on an island, with his hamstring severed to prevent his escape, and ordered to make the king armour and ornaments. In revenge he raped the king's daughter

The legend of the invisible smith living in the barrow called Wayland's Smithy was first recorded by Francis Wise in a letter written in 1738: 'At this place lived formerly an invisible smith: and if a traveller's horse had lost a shoe upon the road, he had no more to do than bring the horse to this place, with a piece of money and leaving both there for some time, he might come again and find the money gone but the horse now shod.'

and, after murdering the king's sons, made goblets from their skulls, which he presented to the king. He escaped using magic wings he had made, he and his wife were reunited and he became a demi-god. It is said that his bones were never entombed in any earthly grave.

Sir Walter Scott incorporated the story of the invisible smith into his novel *Kenilworth*:

'Here are we at Wayland Smith's forge-door.'
'You jest, my little friend,' said Tressilian; 'here is nothing but a bare moor, and that ring of stones, with a great one in the midst, like a Cornish barrow.'
'Ay, and that great flat stone in the midst, which lies across the top of these uprights,' said the boy, 'is Wayland Smith's counter, that you must tell down your money upon … you must tie your horse to that stone which has a ring in't, and then you must whistle three times, and lay me down your silver groat on that other flat stone, walk out of the circle, sit down on the west side of that little thicket of bushes, and take heed you shall neither look to right nor to left for ten minutes, or so long as you shall hear the hammer clink, and whenever it ceases, say your prayers for the space you could tell a hundred – or count over a hundred, which will do as well – and then come into the circle; you will find your money gone and your horse shod.'

Wayland had an assistant called Flibbertigibbet who was once sent to purchase horseshoe nails. The naughty imp tarried birds nesting instead. After waiting for two hours Wayland became impatient, as he had a horse waiting to be shod, so he searched for the imp and on seeing him grabbing a nest twelve miles away he hurled his anvil stone at him. The stone did not quite reach Flibbertigibbet but as it slid along the ground it hit his heel, and he started crying, so the place was named Snivelling Corner. The standing stone at the site was destroyed around 1940.

In the late eighteenth century Job Cork, a shepherd of Uffington, described a different Wayland: Lancelot Wayland, an alchemist's assistant who had an underground laboratory at the barrow which was blown up with gunpowder:

> … At last he was found out, they say,
> He blew up the place and vlod away.
> To Devonshire he then did go,
> Full of sorrow, grief and woe.

Wayland's Smithy has been associated with witchcraft, and a witch's moondial found there in the 1930s was given to Coventry Museum.

The Ridgeway and Icknield Way

The prehistoric Ridgeway on which Wayland's Smithy stands probably dates from at least the Bronze Age, although the route it follows has altered. A legend suggests that somewhere between Wayland's Smithy and the Uffington White Horse a golden coffin is buried, and there is said to be an underground passage linking the smithy with a coomb near Ashbury.

The Icknield Way, another ancient road, was once used as a drovers' road, locally known as Ickleton Road. Local people maintained that it led to the 'World's End' and that you could follow the road all the way round the world and return to the place where you started, but they may just have meant a village of that name near Beedon in Berkshire. A Watlington man is said to have travelled so far along the road that he reached fiery mountains and had to retreat before he was suffocated by the fumes.

Grim's Ditches

Several areas are known as Grim's Ditch or Devil's Ditch near Streatley, Crowmarsh and Nuffield in south Oxfordshire, and at Ardington and Hendred, Aston Upthorpe and Blewbury (the latter also known as Dragon's Ridge), in the Vale of White Horse, probably dating either from the Iron Age or Dark Ages. The Devil was said to have created them while ploughing in a single night, and round barrows nearby were lumps of soil from his ploughshare, and a small mound near Blewbury was hurled at the imp helping him when he ploughed crookedly.

Uffington White Horse

One of the most striking sites is the Uffington White Horse, set high on the hill close to the Ridgeway in the Vale of White Horse. Its date has been a source of controversy for years, some people maintaining that it must be Iron Age

The Uffington White Horse was regarded as a miraculous place in the eleventh century, when the horse was described as having a foal (the only reference to this), and has been considered one of the wonders of Britain for centuries. (Drawing from Thomas Hughes' *The Scouring of the White Horse*, 1859)

because the horse's shape is similar to that on coins of the Dobunni and Atrebates, others that it was a Saxon memorial to King Alfred's victories against the Danes, particularly at the Battle of Ashdown. Legend says that barrows on White Horse Hill house the burials of heroes killed in that battle in AD 871 and it is possible that Neolithic and Bronze Age barrows may have been reused by the Saxons. However, recent excavations have proved that it is the oldest hill figure in England. Optically-stimulated luminescence applied to sediment samples from the horse's belly have given a probable date of 1740-210 BC, with a 68 per cent likelihood that it dates from 1380-550 BC, making it late Bronze Age or early Iron Age. It is unusual in that it faces to the right, unlike most other hill figures, and that it is a silhouette rather than linear shape. The horse is 374ft long, 110ft high and consists of trenches 5-10ft wide and 2-3ft deep with a surface of puddled chalk. Surprisingly, despite being scoured to keep it clean over thousands of years, it has hardly changed shape, although its angle has altered from 18 degrees from horizontal to 8 degrees, making it less easily seen from below.

Most people believe it is a stylised horse, created at a time when the horse was being domesticated, and was a valuable symbol of power. Others suggest that it is a dragon, because of the legend that St George fought and killed the dragon on the flat-topped hill known as Dragon Hill below the figure. An alternative suggestion, made by antiquarian John Aubrey, is that the hill was named after Uther Pendragon, who was killed in battle by the Saxons, and perhaps buried there. Aubrey also postulated a connection with the Anglo-Saxon chieftains Hengist and Horsa, whose names meant 'horse', and suggested they may have had a white horse symbol on their standards. Francis Wise, writing in 1730 reiterated the idea of it being created by Hengist, and added that the local people thought that the horse had moved up the hill.

The horse is close to the Ridgeway, a major prehistoric routeway, and may have marked a site of special significance, a tribal boundary, or a ritual site, or indicated the wealth and power of the local inhabitants. Animals were often used to mark sacred places, ward off evil spirits or encourage fertility. It has also been suggested that it may be associated with the idea of resurrection and victory over death. Even today it is said that it is lucky to stand in the eye of the horse and make a wish, although this is probably not encouraged by its custodians.

The horse has been carefully maintained, or scoured, over the centuries. Thomas Baskerville wrote in 1681 in *Journal of Travels* that it was the 'obligation of some that dwell hereabout to repair and cleanse … the White Horse.' Francis Wise commented in 1736 that 'the ceremony of scouring the Horse, from time immemorial, has been solemnised by a numerous concourse of people from all the villages round about. I am informed, though the horse stands in the parish of Uffington, yet other towns claim, by ancient custom, a share of the duty upon this occasion.' As well as the practical element of scouring, it was a time for fun and games, as described in the *Reading Mercury* of 22 May 1780:

> The ceremony of scouring and cleansing … the White Horse was celebrated on Whit Monday, with great joyous festivity. Besides the customary diversions of horse-racing, foot races etc., many uncommon rural diversions and feats of activity were exhibited to a greater number of spectators than ever assembled on any former occasion. Upwards of thirty thousand persons were present, and amongst them most

Dragon Hill, a small flat-topped hill below the Uffington White Horse, has a 'bald spot' where nothing will grow, said to have been poisoned by the dragon's blood when St George killed it. Some say the dragon's body is buried in the hill.

Wall painting of St George in Hornton church. Some people have suggested that the Uffington White Horse is really a dragon, because the hill below it is called Dragon Hill.

of the nobility and gentry of this and the neighbouring counties; and the whole was concluded without any material accident.

The most famous scouring was on 17 and 18 September 1857, immortalised by Thomas Hughes in *The Scouring of the White Horse* (1859). Booths and stalls in Uffington Castle, the hillfort above the horse, sold apples, nuts, gingerbread, food and drink, fripperies such as ribbons, braces and toys. There were shows, drinking booths, skittle games and a greasy pole to climb (for a leg of mutton), with competitions for backsword play, wrestling, jingling, foot and hurdle races, a carthorse race (for a prize of a harness), a donkey race (for a flitch of bacon), racing down the Manger (for cheeses) and a pig to be chased (the prize of the man who caught him).

During the Second World War the White Horse was such a prominent landmark for invading Germans that it was camouflaged with turf, hedge-trimmings and box trees, fastened down with netting which was not easy to remove after the war so another scouring was performed between 1951 and 1953. Scouring was done again in 2000 to mark the Millennium.

The dip below the hill is known as the Manger, where the horse is said to feed on moonlit nights. The wide curves on one side of the manger are known as the Giant's Stairs. Uffington Castle, the Iron Age hillfort is said to have been used by King Alfred before the Battle of Ashdown.

Ashbury Mystic Circle and Sarsen Stones

At Ashbury the parish church is said to stand within a mystic circle, partly indicated by sarsen stones lining the west side of the churchyard, which some believe suggest that the church was built in the centre of a prehistoric sanctuary similar to that at Avebury. Sarsen stones in nearby fields are said to be sheep petrified by Merlin, King Arthur's magician, or are termed Druid Stones. Large fragments of stone on Chastleton Hill were known as the Grey Geese, and the tale goes that a witch was driving her geese along the lane when they scattered on reaching the hill and she could not get them back together, so in a rage turned them to stone. A large sarsen stone near Bampton is known as the Pudding Stone. It was considered unlucky to move any of the Bampton sarsens.

Shotover Giant

A figure of a giant was cut on the slopes of Shotover Hill, near Oxford, in the seventeenth century before the Civil War. The giant may have held a bow or staff, but no drawing survives. It was nicknamed the Giant Bullingdon, after a nearby common, and his fame was recorded in a poem by Thomas Gillet:

> The giant stood beneath the hill
> And strained his tough bow string so well
> The arrow wandered full three mile
> Onward due east before it fell.

Memories of the lost Shotover Giant hill figure survive in the so-called Giant's Marbles; large spherical stones found on Shotover which he is said to have hurled great distances.

The poet makes the giant help the Britons against Saxon invaders, who are put to flight, but the giant is mortally wounded:

> The peasant finds him on the heath,
> And in the green turf carves his form;
> And while his ashes fade beneath,
> Renews it at each spring's return.

This suggests that there was a similar scouring to that of the White Horse. A long mound, about 60ft long and 5ft wide, probably a Neolithic chamber tomb which stood on Shotover Plain, known as the Giant's Grave, was demolished during tank practice in the course of the Second World War.

The place name Shotover has inspired tales. In 1894 it was said that a certain Harry Bear lived in Headington, close to a quarry bearing his name, and that his friend Lears Hill, who lived at Lye Hill near Wheatley, shot an arrow over the hill to Harry's house when he wanted to talk to him, hence Shotover, or else Harry shot an arrow to Littleworth. There is a type of fossil found in the local ragstone known as 'Harry Bear's beard'. Another tale credits Oliver Cromwell with firing his musket over the hill.

Mazes

Mazes are more recent monuments in the landscape. Although the maze shape had mystical significance as far back as the Bronze Age, some turf mazes may have Roman origins, but most are more likely to be of medieval date (they were often designed for church floors in the twelfth century). Their uses are obscure, but they may have been significant in fertility and funeral rites, for dances and possibly penitential purposes. The only old maze surviving in Oxfordshire is Troy Town at Somerton.

Plan of the spirally designed Troy Maze at Somerton from Top Oxon, which is 50ft by 57ft with a turf path 12in wide and 400 yards long. It is similar in design to one on the floor of Toussaints Abbey in France and another at Dalby in Yorkshire.

Place names such as Muswell Hill near Piddington, which has a square turfed earthwork at the summit surrounded by a low bank known as The Wilderness indicate other possible mazes which have now disappeared. There was a circular maze at Bullingdon known as Tarrytowns or Troytowns, and a turf maze at Tadmarton Heath.

Decorative mazes were constructed in Tudor gardens, and some have been created recently, as at Blenheim Palace, where the Marlborough Maze, designed by Randall Coate and Adrian Fisher uses hedges in a design inspired by Grinling Gibbons' carvings on the palace roof depicting Victory, featuring piles of cannon balls, flags, banners and trumpets and wooden bridges to give a three dimensional puzzle element. It measures 294ft by 158ft.

The Archbishop's Maze at Greys Court, which is 85ft in diameter, was designed in 1981 by Randall Coate and Adrian Fisher for Lady Brunner, inspired by Dr Robert Runcie's enthronement speech when he became Archbishop of Canterbury in which he described a dream where he saw people close to the centre of a maze who could not find their way through and others standing further away who would reach the centre sooner. It is cruciform with Christian symbolism including the crown of thorns, the creation, the nine hours of agony and the twelve apostles. It symbolises the Protestant, Catholic and Orthodox churches, and is a puzzle maze with junctions at which one has to choose a path, representing the paths of life with a multicursal and a unicursal route.

The Troy Maze at Somerton, which used to be visited by children on May Morning. Troy is a common name for mazes. The path may have been followed by penitents.

The Archbishop's Maze at Greys Court, Henley, conceived by Lady Brunner, and based on Robert Runcie's dream before he became Archbishop of Canterbury in 1981. It has brick paths with unicursal and multicursal elements.

Cuckoo Pens

South Oxfordshire particularly is rife with legends about Cuckoo Pens. The arrival of the cuckoo heralded summer, and in folk tales villagers made pens to trap the cuckoo so that it could not escape to stop summer ending as it flew away. At Wittenham Clumps the group of beech trees on Sinodun Hill is known as the Cuckoo Pen. The pen at Benson was a piece of wasteground, at Crowell it was a copse, at Ewelme it was a circle of beech trees, at Idbury it was an enclosed hill, at Ipsden it was an earthen circle planted with tall fir trees, at Swyncombe it was a triangle enclosed by dykes and planted with beech trees, at Warborough the site was a large orchard, and at Watlington it was a circular earthwork 200 yards in circumference planted with beech and plane trees on Shirburn Hill.

two

HISTORICAL LEGENDS

Legends add colour to historical events and places, although they may have no more than a kernel of truth, if that. Oxfordshire has many such legends stretching through the centuries.

The Mapledurham Treasure

There is a fragmentary tradition of a group of Roman soldiers travelling near Mapledurham with an overloaded packhorse who disappeared, presumably drowned or murdered, and another of a packhorse laden with money to pay Roman soldiers which drowned in a flood at Mapledurham lock. There may have been several such incidents. One version maintains that the treasure consisted of eight metal bars, possibly gold, each about 9in long with tapered ends the diameter of a penny, wrapped in oxhide lashed with leather thongs. Another version mentions rings, chains, buckles and brooches revealed where lashings have broken, and a third tells of three sodden leather bags, two intact, the third rotted to reveal silver and gold coins. Vivid dreams, possibly going back to the 1470s, have featured these stories over a cycle of twenty-five to thirty years, particularly among the gypsy community. The dream was reported between 1900 and 1912 in Taunton Deane in Somerset, Theale and Thame. It appeared again in the 1940s in Buckinghamshire, Exmoor and Elstree and in 1968 in Weston-super-Mare, London and Chagford, Devon. Despite the extent of local lore, the treasure has never been found, and it is considered unlucky to talk about the dreams.

St Birinus

Christianity came early to Oxfordshire, with its conversion by St Birinus, who was sent to England by Pope Honorius I in AD 634, where he converted King Cynegils of Wessex who made him Bishop of Dorchester-on-Thames. The saint is said to have preached his first sermon at Churn Knob near Blewbury. He died in AD 650, allegedly as the result of a snake bite. It is said that 'Within the sound of the great bell, no snake nor adder e'er shall dwell' referring to a bell cast in

1380 in Dorchester Abbey which has the inscription *Protégé Birine quos convoco tu sine fine* (Protect Birinus, those whom I call for ever).

St Birinus' bones were removed to Winchester, but in the Middle Ages the monks of Dorchester maintained vociferously that the wrong bones had been moved, and that they still housed the authentic ones. The Archbishop of Canterbury agreed that Dorchester had the genuine bones so the abbey became a centre of pilgrimage. Fragments of the medieval shrine, which was destroyed at the Reformation, have been incorporated into the modern shrine in Dorchester Abbey.

St Frideswide

St Frideswide was probably an Anglo-Saxon princess, perhaps the daughter of Didan, a local sub-king around AD 727, and Safrida. Her tutor Algiva gave her a great love of religion and Frideswide became a nun in the monastery Didan built for her. However, according to twelfth-century legends, after Didan's death she was sought in marriage by Algar, King of Leicester, who threatened to put her in a brothel if she refused him. Algar's envoys were struck blind when they pursued her, but she prayed for them and their sight was restored. Algar himself came to claim her so she fled Oxford after an angel told her to go with two companions to the River Thames where she would find a boat and boatman to rescue her. The boat took her to Bampton, where she sheltered in an abandoned swineherd's hut in a wood. Algar arrived in Oxford and threatened to sack the city if he was

St Frideswide depicted on a thirteenth-century seal of the priory named after her, holding a flower and an open book. In the twelfth century, Augustinian canons trying to exhume her bones were devastated to find an empty coffin, but on digging deeper discovered them. At that moment their torches went out and were miraculously relit; other miracles followed, and the bones were translated to her shrine on 12 February 1180, which became her feast day.

The legend of St Frideswide and Prince Algar as depicted at the Oxford Pageant of 1907.

not informed of her whereabouts, but he in turn was struck blind and returned home. Frideswide hid for three years during which time she performed several miracles including curing a blind girl by washing her eyes with water in which she herself had washed her hands, curing the injury of a young man who had an axe sticking in his hand after working on a Sunday, and restoring the senses of Leowin, a fisherman maddened by demons. She moved to Thornbiri near Binsey and built an oratory, finally returning to her monastery in Oxford, dying shortly afterwards of a fever. More people were cured as she was carried to her grave in St Mary's church, which was subsequently burnt down in the massacre of the Danes in Oxford in 1002 during the reign of King Ethelred.

An alternative tale said that although the weather was icy when she fled, the Hinksey stream refused to freeze, and after she had crossed, the strong current broke the bridge, guarding her route. A spell was cast over the area so that anyone walking through the village would be swallowed up in a marsh and the bridge would never be restored. The locals made a stone causeway, but Wayland the Smith, who had a good trade re-shoeing horses which had lost shoes in the marsh, moved the stones overnight and built a wall to prevent people from prying over White Horse Hill.

Although many details of Frideswide's story are spurious, elements fit in with Anglo-Saxon society, although there is no actual proof of the names of the characters. Her shrine in Christchurch Cathedral, Oxford, is said to be built on the site of her original monastery.

King Alfred

Perhaps the most famous Anglo-Saxon king is King Alfred, who was born in Wantage (where he is commemorated by a Victorian statue in the Market Place), and became king of Wessex in AD 871, spending much of his reign fighting the Danes. Local tradition holds that he fought them at Buckland in a field called 'The Gore' after all the blood that was spilt. A cowherd blew his horn to warn of the Danes' approach, the Blowing Stone was blown, and Alfred and his men were driven back through Hatford to Stanford. At Honeycomb Hill, near the Abingdon to Faringdon road, the Danes refreshed themselves with honey. Later the English pushed them back as far as Gainfield where the Danish leader abandoned his armour to flee across the river (this armour is now said to be in the Ashmolean Museum). However much if not all of this is legend: the word gore comes from the Anglo-Saxon 'gara', a triangle of ploughland, but the story indicates how later people wove stories to explain placenames.

On speech day at King Alfred's School, Wantage, until about 1900, a tray of burnt cakes was carried through the hall to the President of the Old Alfredians Club who said:

President: 'What have ye there?'
Bearer: 'The symbol of a legendary event in the life of our Founder.'
President: 'What other deeds of our Founder do we record?'
Bearer: 'Alfred the Great found learning dead, and he restored it; education neglected

The Blowing Stone at Kingston Lisle has many holes which emit a loud noise when blown correctly. It is claimed to have been used to summon men to King Alfred's army and warn local people of danger. It was probably brought down from nearby hills by Squire Atkins of Kingston Park.

and he revived it; the laws powerless, and he gave them force; the church debased, and he raised it; the land ravaged by a fearful enemy, from which he delivered it. Alfred's name shall live as long as mankind shall respect the past.'

President: 'Alfredians past and present, I call upon you to rise and sing the praises of Alfred, our Royal Founder.'

(Quoted in S. Jackson Coleman, *Tales and Traditions of Berkshire*, 1949)

King Canute

Eventually the Danes did conquer England, which was ruled by King Canute from 1016-35 after he defeated the Anglo-Saxon King Edmund Ironside. Local tradition says that that Edmund was the victor in a battle at Sarsden in 1016 – if so, it was not important enough to have featured in history books.

There are conflicting traditions concerning the Pusey horn. One version says that a shepherd boy saw the Danish army and used his cow horn to warn his employers, which saved the house from being captured. The boy was well rewarded, and his horn kept at the Manor and handed down from one generation to the next. Another version suggests the horn was blown by a man named Pusey to warn King Canute of an ambush, and was rewarded by a gift of the lands at Pusey. As token of ownership King Canute presented him with a horn inscribed 'Kynge Knoud geve Wyllyam Pewse thys horne to holde by thy Londe.' The horn is dark brown, about 2ft 6in long with a maximum circumference of 1ft. Later generations mounted it in ornate silver gilt with legs and a dog's head decoration which could be moved to convert it from a hunting horn to a drinking horn. It was shown to Judge Jeffries in the Court of Chancery in the seventeenth century to establish ownership of Pusey in a lawsuit, and eventually given to the Victoria & Albert Museum. However, it is said to have been presented around AD 665, four centuries before Canute reigned.

Edward the Confessor

Edward the Confessor was born in Islip in 1004, and there is an octagonal font, now at Middleton Stoney, which is said to have come from the royal palace of Islip, engraved with the words:

> This sacred font St Edward first receav'd
> From womb to grace, from grace to glory went;
> His virtuous life to this fayre isle bequeathed,
> Prase … and to us but lent.
> Let this remaine the trophies of his fame,
> A king baptiz'd from hence a saint became.

The font is fourteenth century, but may have been re-carved from an earlier font, and the inscription dates from the seventeenth century.

A font, now in Middleton Stoney church, which may have come from the royal palace of Islip, with an inscription commemorating Edward the Confessor.

William the Conqueror

William the Conqueror is said to have stayed in Banbury at the Altarstone Inn in Bridge Street, so named after a stone depicting a ram and a fire which stood in a niche under the sign which may have been from a Roman altar.

Robin Hood

Many legends about Robin Hood, the famous outlaw, date from the reigns of Richard I and King John. One ballad, quoted in Alfred Beesley's *History of Banbury* (1841) relates:

> How Robin by a wile
> The Tinker he did cheat;
> But at the length as you shall hear
> The tinker did him beat,
> Whereby the same they did then so agree
> They after lived in love and unity.

Robin was on his way to Nottingham when he met a tinker who said:

> I am a tinker by my trade,
> And do live at Banbura.

Robin asks what news the tinker has, and he replies:

> It is to seek a bold outlaw,
> Which they call Robin Hood.
> I have a warrand from the King,
> To take him where I can;
> If you can tell me where hee is,
> I will make you a man.
> The King would give a hundred pound,
> That he could but him see…

Robin replies:

> 'Let me see that warrant', said Robin Hood,
> 'Ile see if it bee right;
> And I will do the best I can
> For to take him this night.'

The tinker refused and they proceeded to Nottingham together to look for the outlaw, where the tinker got drunk and Robin disappeared, taking the tinker's warrant and money, but leaving him to pay the bill. The innkeeper informed him that his companion had been the notorious Robin himself, so the tinker left his tools as token of his honest intent and left in hot pursuit:

> At last hee spy'd him in a park,
> Hunting then of the deer.
> 'What knave is that', quoth Robin Hood,
> 'That doth come mee so near?'
> 'No knave, no knave' the Tinker said,
> 'And that you soon shall know;
> Whether of us hath done any wrong,
> My crab-tree shaft shall show.'

They fought, and Robin yielded, but while the tinker caught his breath Robin blew his horn and Little John and Will Scadlock came to his aid. Knowing that he was now safe, Robin offered to give the tinker a hundred pounds a year, saying:

> In manhood he is a mettled man,
> And mettle man by trade;
> Never thought I that any man
> Should have made mee so afraid.
> And if hee will bee one of us,
> Wee will take all one fare;
> And whatsoever wee do get,
> He shall have his full share.'
> So the Tinker was content
> With them to go along,

And with them a part to take:
And so I end my song.

Queen Matilda's Escape

Matilda had her headquarters in Oxford during her civil war with Stephen in 1141. She was besieged in Oxford Castle for three months and stores ran low. As there was snow it was difficult to escape unnoticed so she and her followers dressed in white and slipped out, travelling up the frozen Thames to Abingdon, then on to the safety of Wallingford Castle.

Henry II

A pub at Goring, the Miller of Mansfield, commemorates a story about how King Henry II became lost while out hunting and took shelter, without revealing his identity, at a mill. The miller gave him a venison pie, confessing that the deer had been poached from the royal forest and woe betide him if the King ever found out! Henry was so amused that he gave the miller a well paid job as king's forester.

Henry often stayed at the royal hunting lodge at Woodstock, which he made into a palace. He is said to have secreted his beloved mistress Rosamund de Clifford, his favourite for about eleven years before her death in 1176, in a maze here, to protect her from the wrath of his jealous wife Eleanor of Aquitaine. He

Henry II depicted with Fair Rosamund de Clifford, his beloved mistress for many years, in a scene from the Oxford Pageant.

certainly built a bower here near the Everswell spring which is known as Fair Rosamund's Well, although there is no contemporary evidence that she stayed there. The first reference to it came in Ranulf Higden's *Polychronicon* in 1387:

> To this fair wench the King made at Woodstock a chamber of wonder craft, wonderly made by Daedalus' work, lest the Queen should find and take Rosamund.

According to legend Henry once caught one of Rosamund's embroidery silks on his spur as he left her, which unravelled to provide the key to the maze, which was followed by Eleanor who, according to sixteenth-century ballads, confronted her rival, giving her the choice of death by poison or incarceration in the nearby Godstow nunnery. It is fact that Rosamund went to Godstow before her death, possibly because she was ill and required nursing. Eleanor could not have murdered her, because her husband was keeping her in prison. This did not stop lurid stories arising, such as the fourteenth-century French *Chronicle of London* which claimed that Eleanor stripped Rosamund, roasted her naked between two fires, put venomous toads on her breasts and bled her to death in a hot bath at Woodstock. This story was full of inaccuracies, as it named her as Eleanor of Provence, not of Aquitaine (the title of Henry III's wife), and made the date of the murder 1262 instead of 1176.

Rosamund was lavishly buried in the choir of Godstow nunnery, which received much money from Henry II. The nuns were proud of her tomb, which was covered by a silken pall, and lit by candles. When Bishop Hugh of Lincoln visited Godstow in 1191 he was horrified to see the tomb and responded, 'Take her away from here, for she was a harlot, and bury her outside of the church with

Woodstock Palace, where Henry II may have designed the enclosed pools and orchards for Rosamund de Clifford, possibly based on the romance of Tristan and Iseult, or influenced by the Arab-inspired pavilions and water gardens of the Kings of Sicily.

the rest, that the Christian religion may not grow into contempt and that other women, warned by her example, may abstain from illicit and adulterous intercourse.' Rosamund was reburied in the chapter house, and her tomb inscribed:

> Hic jacet in tumba rosa mundi, non rosa munda;
> Non redolet, sed olet, quae redolere solet.

This translates as:

> Here lies the rose of the world, not a clean rose;
> She no longer smells rosy, so hold your nose.

Ranulf Higden described the tomb as being about 2ft long, decorated with giants and animals. John Leland described the tomb's destruction in the sixteenth century: 'Rosamund's tomb at Godstow was taken up [of] late; it is a stone with this inscription 'Tomba Rosamundae'. Her bones were closed in lead, and within that in leather. When it was opened a very sweet smell came out of it.'

Another story says a nut tree grew over her grave but its roots were poisoned so the nutshells had no kernels. Her story lingered on to be described in a sixteenth-century ballad, published in Percy's *Reliques*:

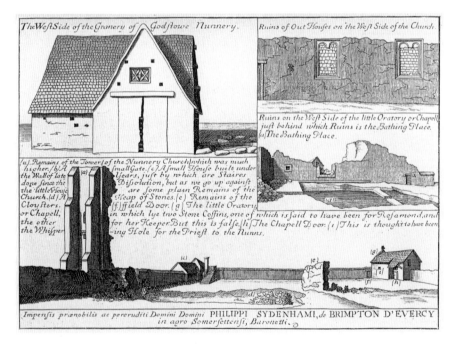

Engraving of the ruins of Godstow Abbey, where Fair Rosamund was buried. According to legend, when Henry II came to view her body he was shocked to see, when the tomb was opened, that a large toad sat between her breasts and an adder coiled round her waist, and the smell was nauseating.

Most curiously that bower was built
Of stone and timber strong,
An hundred and fifty doors
Did to this bower belong.
And they so cunninglye continu'd
With turnings round about,
That none but with a clue of thread
Could enter in or out.

Minster Lovell Legends

Several legends are attached to the picturesque medieval ruins of Minster Lovell.
Francis, Lord Lovell, was a close friend of Richard III, who awarded him the post
of Constable of the Royal Castle of Wallingford and Chamberlain of the Royal
Household when he was in his twenties. Others became jealous, leading to the
rhyme:

The catte, the ratte and Lovell our dogge
Rule all England under the hogge.

Ruins of Minster Lovell Hall,
where, according to tradition,
Lord Lovell's former valet, Rustling
Jack, wanted to find his master's
treasure, so he, Tobias the monk,
Pentecost, and two local women
dug up the dovecote floor and
descended into a secret chamber
where they found the skeleton of
Lord Lovell seated at a table with
pen and paper, with his faithful
hound at his feet, all of which
crumbled to dust before their eyes.
(Drawing from Alfred Rimmer's
Pleasant Spots Around Oxford,
1878)

Lovell's nickname came from his badge, a Talbot hound; the rat was Sir Richard Ratcliffe, the cat Sir William Catesby, and Richard III was named after his badge, the boar. Lovell fled to Flanders after Richard's death at the Battle of Bosworth, returning to England to support Lambert Simnel's revolt, and was last seen in 1487 swimming his horse across the River Trent after the Battle of Stoke. An inquisition was held into his fate and decided that he had escaped and died abroad, although there was no evidence to support this. However, local tradition asserts that he rode back to Minster Lovell, where a faithful servant hid him, perhaps for several years, in a secret chamber, but that the servant died suddenly and as no-one else knew he was there, Lovell was left to starve.

William Cowper, Clerk to Parliament, wrote in 1737 that in 1708 workmen discovered a secret vault behind an old chimney and inside was the skeleton of a man seated at a table with a book, pen and paper with his dog at his feet, and a cap lying on the floor but that the bones crumbled to dust before their eyes. The same story is also attached to Upton Lovell in Wiltshire.

Minster Lovell ruins are haunted by a knight in shining armour on a white charger, perhaps the hapless Francis Lord Lovell whose ghost perhaps makes the groans and sounds of rustling papers said to come from underground.

Another sad story attached to the Lovell family is related in a ballad:

> The mistletoe hung in the castle hall,
> The holly bush shone on the old oak wall;
> The baron's retainers were blithe and gay
> Keeping their Christmas holiday.
> The baron beheld with a father's pride,
> His beautiful child, Lord Lovell's bride;
> While she with her bright eyes seemed to be
> The star of that goodly company.
> O, the mistletoe bough.
>
> 'I'm weary of dancing now', she cried,
> 'Here tarry a moment, I'll hide, I'll hide;
> And Lovell, be sure thou'rt first to trace
> The clue to my secret hiding place'.
>
> Away she went, and her friends began
> Each tower to search and each nook to scan,
> And Lord Lovell cried, 'O, where doest thou hide?
> I'm lonesome without thee my own dear bride.'
> O, the mistletoe bough.
>
> They sought her that night, and they sought her next day;
> They sought her in vain till a week passed away,
> In the highest, the lowest, the loneliest spot,
> Young Lovell sought wildly, but found her not.
> And years flew by, and their grief at last
> Was told as a sorrowful tale long past.
> And when Lovell appeared the children cried,

'See the old man weeps for his fairy bride.'
O, the mistletoe bough.

At length an old chest that had long been hid,
Was found in the castle – they raised the lid;
And a skeletal form lay mouldering there
In the bridal wreath of a lady fair.
O, sad was her fate, in sportive jest,
She hid from her lord in the old oak chest.
It closed with a spring, and her bridal bloom
Lay withering there in a living tomb.
O, the mistletoe bough.

A number of chests, each claiming to be the authentic mistletoe bough chest, have been sold at auction over the years, and one is displayed at Greys Court, near Henley-on-Thames. The same story has also been attached to houses at Bramshill in Hampshire, Dalby Hall near Melton and Exton Hall, but it seems to have originated in fifteenth-century Italy and it is unlikely that any unfortunate bride lost her life in this way at Minster Lovell.

Another story relates that a certain Lovell came to Minster Lovell where he fell for his brother's wife and in his jealousy shot him. The widow refused to have anything to do with her brother-in-law, and in her grief drowned herself in what is now known as the Lady's Pool. The brother in his furious grief burnt down the house and when workmen tried to demolish the ruins their axes broke.

Amy Robsart

Amy Robsart, the neglected wife of Sir Robert Dudley, favourite of Queen Elizabeth I, spent her last days in 1560 staying at Cumnor Place with Anthony Forster and his wife and Mrs William Owen, wife of the house's owner. On 8 September Lady Dudley sent the servants to Abingdon Fair and when they returned they discovered her body at the bottom of the stairs, her neck broken. She had not been alone, but no-one was able to explain how she had fallen. It was later suggested that she may have had breast cancer, which could have weakened her bones, or that she may have been so distraught at her husband's neglect that she committed suicide, or that her existence was interfering with Robert's chances with Queen Elizabeth, so he arranged for her to be pushed. The truth will probably never be known. Dudley showed no grief on hearing of her death, but although the jury returned a verdict of mischance or accidental death, his reputation was tarnished. In 1567 Amy's half-brother declared that the jury had been suborned and that she had been murdered, but when brought before the Privy Council he confessed to bringing a false charge.

Cumnor Place, where Amy Robsart, wife of Sir Robert Dudley, fell down the stairs to her death. Her beautiful, magnificently attired ghost haunted the house, but was laid to rest by nine or twelve parsons in a pool, later known as Madam Dudley's Pool, which is said never to have frozen since.

The funeral of Amy Robsart as depicted for the Oxford Pageant of 1907. She was buried in the church of St Mary the Virgin in High Street, Oxford. Her ghost appeared as a death omen to Robert Dudley at Combury Park in 1588, and has appeared there since, while his ghost has been seen at Ditchley.

The Civil War

Many stories attach to the traumatic period of the Civil War. The ghost of Archbishop Laud, a favourite of Charles I, who was executed in 1645, has been seen rolling its head round the library of St John's College. St John's has a portrait of Charles I entirely made up from minute quotations from the psalms, with phrases used for eyebrows and entire psalms for his moustache and beard. Charles is said to have coveted this and offered the College anything it desired in return for the portrait, but to his dismay their wish was to keep it.

Lord Saye and Sele of Broughton Castle and his sons fought for Parliament at the first battle of the war at Edgehill, on the Oxfordshire/Warwickshire border in October 1642. The battle was indecisive, but afterwards contemporary pamphlets reported violent apparitions around Edgehill, reprinted in Alfred Beesley's *History of Banbury*:

> … In which place is heard and seene fearfull and strange apparitions of spirits as sounds of drums, trumpets. With the discharging of Canons and Muskies, Carbines, pettronels, to the terrour and amazement of all the fearfull hearers and beholders… Whose dying grones a second time revives breaking the caverns of the couring earth, and sends both feare and horour round about to terrifie the living with dead souls.

The effigy of Sir Robert Dudley and his second wife Lettice in St Mary's church, Warwick.

Lord Saye and Sele and fellow conspirators gathered in an upper tower room at Broughton Castle, which had only one easily guarded entrance, to plot secretly against Charles I before the Civil War without fear of being overheard.

The battle seemed to be refought in the sky, with sound and lights. Men from both sides came to investigate and discovered that some of the bodies had not been buried properly. After this had been remedied the sounds died down, but the ghostly army is said to reappear on the anniversary of the battle, and police dogs patrolling around Edgehill on that day refuse to go to certain areas.

At the 1643 Battle of Chalgrove Field locals claimed the Oxford road ran with blood. A woman named Brown set out to milk her cows on the common but was warned that if she did she would be killed. Hungry soldiers are said to have stolen the bread cooking in a local farmhouse oven.

At Chinnor there was said to be a secret staircase in the Black Boy Inn, which Oliver Cromwell once used to make a quick escape. Prince Rupert was said to have been injured in the village, and soldiers' uniforms and the the bones of horses were found under the floorboards in the church, which was used as stables.

On the night of 3 June 1644 King Charles and an army of 6,000 men left Oxford secretly, travelling through Yarnton down Froggledown Lane on their way to Hanborough Bridge. Around the anniversary of the ride the sounds of the passing army have been heard: harness jingling, the clatter of hooves and chatter of the men, but nothing has ever been seen. The ghost of Charles I haunts the old manor house at Sandford-on-Thames, where he once stayed; on the anniversary of his visit the sound of a carriage and horses is heard.

Local lore maintains that when marching towards Oxford in 1644 Oliver Cromwell encountered a fisherman called Beckley who helped ferry the Parliamentary troops across the River Cherwell. When he came to power Cromwell rewarded Beckley by granting him fishing rights over that part of

The memorial to Lucius Cary, Lord Falkland on the Tanfield tomb in Burford church. When Charles I was appalled to divine in Virgil's *Aeneid* an omen of the loss of his kingdom and friends and his own early death, Lord Falkland tried to cheer him by divining his own future, but his own death in battle was foretold. Both divinations proved true: Charles I was executed at the age of forty-nine and Lord Falkland died in 1643 at the Battle of Newbury.

the river. Cromwell sat in the church tower to get an overview of fighting at Islip Bridge on 28 February 1645, where he defeated the Queen's Regiment and troops under the Earl of Northampton.

Arthur Jones of Chastleton House fought for Charles II at the Battle of Worcester in 1651, and fled home afterwards, hotly pursued by Commonwealth soldiers. On hearing their horses in the courtyard, his wife, Sarah, quickly hid Arthur in a room over the parlour which had its secret entrance hidden by tapestries. The soldiers hoped they were about to capture the king, but if not, they wanted Arthur Jones. Being tired and hungry from their ride, they quartered themselves in the house, unwittingly choosing to sleep next to the secret room, where a cough from Arthur would have given away his hiding place. Sarah brought a large jug of ale, to which she had secretly added laudanum, which sent them into a deep sleep, so she could extract Arthur, who took the best of the soldiers' horses and fled to safety before they awoke.

Commonwealth Commissioners commandeered Woodstock Manor in 1647, but were terrorised by royalist Joe Collins who had disguised himself as their secretary, Giles Sharp. The rector, Thomas Widdowes wrote in *The Just Devil of Woodstock*:

> The devil made imaginative use of very simple resources: a little gunpowder tactfully placed; faggots of wood from the famous King's Oak, which the Commissioners had felled as being too monarchical; a black dog, three dozen wooden trenchers, … stones and glass from the wreckage, a warming pan, some horses' bones, and a pail or two of 'green stinking water'. Billets of oak, stones, bones, glass and furniture

Chastleton House, the small window indicating the secret chamber where Arthur Jones successfully hid from Roundhead soldiers after the Battle of Worcester. He escaped, but the family was later crippled by heavy fines.

were flung dangerously about; gunpowder extinguished the candles or exploded in the fire; trenchers 'rolled horribly', or flew at heads; dogs howled and Something walked like a bear... Such manifestations struck such panic into Rumpish breasts and the Commissioners ... withdrew to Ewelme.

The George Inn at Wallingford has a room known as the Tear Drop Room, as it has a pattern of tear drops on the walls. The story goes that the landlord's daughter loved a Royalist sergeant who died after a pub brawl and was so grief-stricken that she locked herself in this room and died broken-hearted, after mixing her tears with soot and painting tear drops on the wall, returning to haunt it.

A Civil War soldier fled from a skirmish to a barn near Church Farm, Towersey, but when his horse neighed was discovered and shot. He was buried in the churchyard under large flat stones. His ghost is seen riding a grey horse between the barn and the graveyard. Dr Oldys, the vicar of Adderbury, was betrayed to Parliamentary troops and, despite scattering his money along the road to delay his pursuers, he was shot. Later his betrayer fell dead on the same spot.

Lord Rochester

In 1659, the notorious John Wilmot, Lord Rochester of Adderbury House, disguised himself as a tinker, but instead of mending pots, destroyed them, later replacing them with new ones. He pretended to be a tramp, and on meeting another tramp who warned that it was no good begging from Lord Rochester, punished him by putting him in a barrel of beer before giving him new clothes and food, warning him not to spread false rumours!

Stephen Rumbold

Stephen Rumbold was a character who died at Brightwell Baldwin in 1687. His epitaph reads:

> He lived one hundred and five
> Sanguine and strong
> An hundred to five
> You don't live so long.

He is commemorated by Rumbold's Lane, Hill and Copse, and remembered for brewing strong beer, and the fact that when quite old he is said to have run off with a young local girl.

Highwaymen

Highwaymen were a hazard to travellers for centuries. Captain James Hind, a saddler's son, was born in 1616 in Chipping Norton, educated at the local grammar school and apprenticed as a butcher. James however wanted a life of adventure and left to seek his fortune in London. After a drunken binge he ended up in prison where he met the highwayman James Allen, and on their release

The highwayman sign at Hopcroft's Holt on the Banbury to Oxford road, the headquarters of Frenchman Claude Duval for about eight years. He had an eye for the ladies and let a pretty lady keep her jewellery if she consented to dance with him. He was hanged at Tyburn around 1820. The Quiet Woman pub at Chipping Norton (now an antiques centre) was run by a deaf and dumb woman and was a haunt for highwaymen who knew she could not give them away.

joined him. Despite travelling the country in the course of his career, he married a Chipping Norton girl, Margaret Rowland, and had four children. Many stories tell of his consideration towards his victims. He held up a countryman near Wantage, who pleaded that he had all his savings with him to buy a cow for his family. Hind responded that he needed the money now, but if the man would meet him at the same place in a week's time, he would give him enough money to buy two cows. He sometimes wore a disguise, and was unrecognised when he robbed a butcher friend, but soon returned the six shillings he had taken plus twenty shillings to buy some gloves.

He became a Royalist captain during the Civil War, and made a point of trying to rob as many Regicides as he could find. He fought for Charles II at the Battle of Worcester, but was captured in 1651 and questioned as a political prisoner at Whitehall. At first he was tried for his Royalist acts, but this accusation was dropped and instead he was charged with highway robbery and sentenced to be hanged, drawn and quartered on 29 September 1652.

Dick Turpin, the notorious highwayman, was based for a while at Manor Farm, Appleford, while holding up travellers on the Oxford to London road. He was later hanged for his crimes in York in 1739. The Methodist John Wesley was accosted at Shotover near Oxford, on the Oxford to London road in 1737; the highwayman, on taking his purse, asked if he had any more money in his pockets. Wesley said that he had not, and the highwayman trusted him as he was a preacher, and left him in peace, although in fact Wesley had lied to him.

The Dunsden brothers, Tom, Dick and Harry, were born of respectable yeomen stock at Fulbrook, the eldest, Richard, in 1745. Apparently an injustice was done to one of the brothers, so they took to the road where they robbed farmers of stock and money, which they hid in various places, including a cave in Wychwood Forest. Then they stole £500 from the Oxford coach. A planned robbery at Tangley Hall went disastrously wrong when their plans got out, and the owners and several constables were lying in wait when the Dunsdens arrived. Dick slid his arm through the lookout shutter of the front door to open the catch. To his horror his arm was grasped firmly from inside and the only way for him to escape was to amputate his arm at the elbow. Dick disappears from the story at this point so probably died from his injury.

Another time they were burying a body early one morning when they were seen by a hedger and ditcher, so they murdered him and buried him in the same grave. They took their shoes to be mended by the shoemaker at Fifield, arriving on horseback at dead of night and leaving the shoes outside his door, returning to collect them another night, leaving a tip as well as the fee.

Tom and Harry shot and mortally wounded a man while gambling at a race meeting at Burford on Whit Sunday 1784 and were overpowered by race-goers. They were convicted at Gloucester and their bodies were gibbeted in cages on an oak tree at Capps Lodge near Fulbrook, where people gathered around the tree on Sunday afternoons to see how much was left of the bodies. The initials 'H.D.' and 'T.D.' and the date 1784 were carved in the bark of the tree.

Poaching Tales

Poaching was potentially punishable by death or blinding in the king's royal hunting forests of Wychwood and Shotover, with harsh laws decreeing that men could be punished even if they had neglected to clip their dogs' claws, but the presence of deer, wild boar, hares and rabbits was a sore temptation. In 1413 scholars of Oxford University made such nuisances of themselves poaching that they were prohibited from entering Woodstock Park. Keepers policed the forest; on one occasion they found a deer's carcase, skinned and ready for market, and confiscated it, but on their way home stopped for a drink at the Crown Inn at Shipton-under-Wychwood, where the locals distracted them by praising their prowess while the carcass was whisked away again by the poachers.

An Ascott-under-Wychwood man shot a deer and rushed home to get his wife to help him haul it onto the back of his horse so that he could sell it in Banbury. They cut off the buck's head and the wife walked home carrying it on her head. That same evening a young man was poaching for the first time, despite his mother's dire warning that he would see the Evil One. As he crept into the forest he saw a figure with antlers on its head and in his terror was convinced that he had seen the Devil. He fled home in panic and was ill for the next fortnight.

The gamekeepers had to resort to cunning to catch poachers. A noted poacher met a stranger, a rough looking young man setting out snares in an amateurish

Poachers often hid their venison in the small rooms above church porches such as this one at Burford, or in secret rooms created inside ricks or false bottoms in carriers' carts.

Bale tombs such as this one in Burford churchyard were used to hide poachers' ill-gotten gains. Sometimes hiding places had to be rapidly improvised: a woman once put a venison pie in the crook of her arm and hid it by placing her baby on top when a keeper arrived on the scene unexpectedly.

way while out poaching, so he showed him the best way to set them. Early next morning he decided to empty the snares before the young man got to them. To his shocked dismay the young man arrived as he was extracting the game, dressed in gamekeeper's uniform and arrested him. Another poacher was cornered on an icy night by gamekeepers and his only escape route was to cross the river, and when he got home his trousers were so frozen to his legs that his wife had to cut them off with scissors.

Sometimes the consequences of poaching were fatal. Despite protesting their innocence two men were convicted of murdering a keeper on circumstantial evidence, and hanged at Oxford. Many years later another poacher confessed that he had shot the keeper, mistaking him for a deer.

In the 1840s large groups of destitute men roamed the countryside, often poaching en route. Lord Dynevore was warned that Black Country men were expected in the area and appealed to Milton poachers to join the keepers in protecting the game. A fight ensued and a man was killed by being hit with a flail but in court it was deemed justifiable homicide.

In the nineteenth century the punishment for transgressors could be transportation, but poachers tried to fight back and produced an anonymous circular which was sent to local gentlemen who would act as magistrates:

TAKE NOTICE – We have lately heard and seen that there is an act passed, and whatever poacher is caught destroying the game is to be transported for seven years. This is English liberty! Now we do swear to each other, that the first of our company that this law is inflicted on, that there shall be not one gentleman's set in our county escape the rage of fire. We are nine in number, and we will burn every gentleman's house of note. The first that impeaches shall be shot. We have sworn not to impeach. You may think it a threat, but they will find it a reality. The Game Laws were too severe before. The Lord of all men sent these animals for the peasants as well as for the prince. God will not let his people be oppressed. He will assist us in our undertaking, and we will execute it with caution.

Most poachers were poorly paid agricultural labourers or quarrymen so poaching would have supplemented their incomes and fed their families. Twenty-eight men were sentenced to death for poaching in 1829.

The Otmoor Riots

Otmoor was a wetland with a close-knit community. The people claimed that 'Our Lady of Otmoor' rode a circuit round the moor while an oatsheaf was burning, and gave the area inside it to the people of Otmoor in perpetuity. In a nineteenth-century pamphlet Sir Alexander Croke, who refuted the validity of the story, said people thought the donor was Elizabeth I or another queen, or King Charles I.

The Otmoor riots were conducted by desperate agricultural labourers who saw the additional sources of income they cherished disappearing as the wetland of Otmoor was enclosed in 1829 and drained to the benefit of the landowners, as a rhyme accused:

> The fault is great in Man or Woman
> Who steals the Goose from off a Common;
> But who can pleas that man's excuse
> Who steals the Common from the Goose.

This refers to the Aylesbury ducks and geese bred on the common land before enclosure. The first drainage attempts were unsuccessful and led to flooding. Nocturnal raids started in 1829 and on 5 June 1830 enclosure banks were attacked and twenty-nine local farmers were charged with breaking the banks of the River Ray and flooding the lands of Sir Alexander Croke. They pleaded that the banks were a public nuisance and were acquitted. The people of Otmoor then believed that the whole enclosure was null and void and they could destroy fences and re-establish their rights of common.

The Revd Philip Searle, Rector of Oddington, was a promoter of the enclosures:

> It was narrow back, the parson,
> As I have heard 'em say,
> Who employed the Parish Clerk
> To stop the River Ray.
> He blocked up the water
> For four feet high or more
> To injure other farmers
> And keep it out of Otmoor.

The rioters blackened their faces, wore women's cloaks, tied black scarves over their heads and armed themselves with billhooks, hatchets, pitchforks and staves. Some nights 20 men, other nights up to 150, set out to destroy hedges and stakes with their billhooks. Attempts were made to keep the situation under control by stationing Coldstream Guards at Islip and additional policemen in the villages, although they could have none at Charlton because no-one would offer them lodgings. The authorities tried to bribe men to inform, leading to the rhyme, which is found in several versions:

> I went to Noke
> And nobody spoke,
> I went to Brill
> They were silent still,
> I went to Thame
> It was just the same,
> I went to Beckley
> They spoke directly.

Robert Graves wrote about the riots in *Antigua Penny Puce*: 'Black men are Oddy born [Oddington], marsh men are called black men. Oddy bells are supposed to ring "Hang Sam Gomme, Save Will Young".'

Sam Gomme was a spy employed by Lord Churchill's Yeomanry and Will Young one of the rioters' ringleaders. Everything came to a head on 6 September 1830 when around 1,000 people perambulated the seven mile circumference of Otmoor in broad daylight, destroying every fence in their way. The Riot Act was read to them, and the Oxfordshire Yeomanry was summoned, but they refused to disperse and sixty-six rioters were arrested, forty-one of whom were loaded aboard wagons to be taken to Oxford Prison escorted by twenty-one yeomen commanded by Captain Hamilton. The magistrates feared conspiracy as handbills had been published by 'the King of Otmoor, Given at our Court of Otmoor'. The rioters were not all local, some coming from Oxford, Bicester and nearby villages. They were not tied up, so when a large mob outside the city attacked the escort with stones and bricks, the prisoners escaped. The situation gradually calmed down and fence-breaking ceased after 1835.

Another 'legend' emerged that the local people had webbed feet, illustrated by a weathervane erected on Charlton church around 1955. The Revd E.H.W. Crusha wrote to Miss Eltenton that he was furious about this: 'It is commonly said that "Otmoor goslings have webbed feet" (or rather Otmoor gollins)… It is as old as the memories of surviving old people… I have myself no doubt that it originated as a kind of insult which "foreigners" used towards Otmoor men.'

The Murder of John Kalabergo

John Kalabergo, an Italian refugee, set up shop in Banbury in the early nineteenth century and reluctantly invited his ne'er-do-well nephew William to work with him. John kept a tight rein over his charge and William grew resentful and bought himself a pistol. One evening in 1852 Kalabergo's horse and trap were found

John Kalabergo, an Italian refugee who had a shop selling clocks, jewellery, thermometers and barometers in Banbury in the early nineteenth century.

John Kalabergo was murdered by his ungrateful nephew on Williamscot Hill. A memorial stone was set up by his friends, which has now been moved to Banbury Museum.

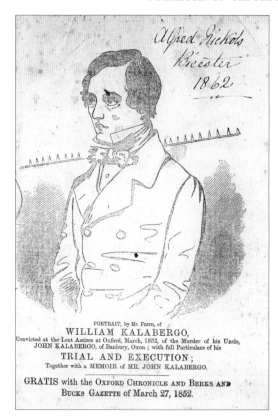

Alfred Nickols Bicester 1862

PORTRAIT, by Mr. Farm, of
WILLIAM KALABERGO,
Convicted at the Lent Assizes at Oxford, March, 1852, of the Murder of his Uncle,
JOHN KALABERGO, of Banbury, Oxon ; with full Particulars of his
TRIAL AND EXECUTION;
Together with a MEMOIR of MR. JOHN KALABERGO.

GRATIS with the OXFORD CHRONICLE AND BERKS AND
BUCKS GAZETTE of March 27, 1852.

The murderer, William Kalabergo,
in dock at Oxford Assizes in 1852.
The drawings are from a supplement
about the trial in the *Oxford Chronicle*
and *Berks and New Bucks Gazette,*
27 March 1852.

abandoned and John Kalabergo's body lay in a pool of blood on Williamscot Hill.
A little later William incoherently told the Revd Tandy, the Catholic priest, that
they had been attacked by robbers. However his explanation was not believed and
he was condemned at the Lent Assizes and hanged in Oxford.

Deddington Pudding Pies

Deddington is famous for its pudding pies which were sold at the Martinmas
Pudding Pie Fairs. They consisted of bread pudding enclosed in a suet crust, but
did not enjoy a very good reputation: it was said that pies were so hard that you
could tie a label to one and send it through the post for a hundred miles, or that
'Deddington folk were supposed to save up all the scrapings from the candle
drippings in the lanterns and put them in the pudding pies.' When a certain king
travelled through Oxfordshire, he was presented with local produce such as cakes
in Banbury and gloves in Woodstock, but at Deddington he was given a compro-
mise between the two, which was rather like leather but not intended to be eaten!
The pies were last made in the 1930s.

Oxfordshire Roads

Crossroads were considered mysterious places; suicides were often buried there so that their unquiet souls would not be able to find their way home. Condive's Corner on the Enstone Road where the parishes of Charlbury and Spelsbury meet is said to be named after a suicide buried there, who was found hanging from a beam in his house in Sheep Street, Charlbury. However, years later, a woman admitted that she had seen someone climbing a ladder into Condive's bedroom that evening and that he might have been murdered, so his body was exhumed and reburied in Charlbury churchyard.

Mary Hill's grave at the crossroads where the Stonefield to Fawler road meets the Northleigh to Ashford road is said to be the grave of a suicide who was buried with a stake through her body. The name dates back at least to 1712. It is possible that the name is a corruption of 'Merry Hill' with a possible association with 'mare' an Old English term for goblin, as there are several ancient sites nearby, and these are often associated in folk memory with goblins.

Pack and Prime, near Henley-on-Thames, leading from Henley to Goring and from the river via Fawley Deer Park to Henley Park were originally pack roads and the name comes from the order given to start off the packhorse train 'pack and prime': pack your goods and prime your pistols.

three

CHURCH LORE

Poor Uffington, proud people,
Has a church without a steeple,
But what is more to its disgrace,
Has a clock without a face.

Until the Reformation the church dominated society, physically as well as mentally. Churches were the most important buildings of the village and the Church exerted influence over almost every aspect of life, with rituals for expulsion of evil spirits, to drive away thunder and bless aspects of life and work. Beliefs

Rows of birds' heads on the west Norman doorway of Iffley church, carved to protect the entrance and ward off demons which were believed to come from the west. Demons were carved in chains to further deter them. Barford St Michael also has a beak-headed door.

were reflected in the architecture and decoration of the churches. Weathervanes often feature a cock, as crowing frightened demons. The small north door was opened during baptism to let the Devil leave the church after being driven out of the baby. Seeing the image of St Christopher was said to offer a day's preservation from illness and death, so many churches had prominent wall-paintings of St Christopher, as at Bloxham, where St Christopher is accompanied by a hermit and a mermaid, facing the principal doorway.

The green man is a controversial character, generally being thought of as a fertility figure, much more pagan in aspect than one would expect to find in a church. Such figures, depicted with greenery erupting from their mouths, are rare in Oxfordshire but there is a detailed foliate mask in Dorchester Abbey.

Church bells formed the framework for the day for ordinary people who had no clocks or watches: on Sunday the 10.00 a.m. bell was taken as the signal to take the joint to be cooked at the bakehouse and the 12.45 p.m. bell was the time to collect it. King Alfred ordered the Curfew bell to be rung at 8.00 p.m. as a sign that it was time to cover the fire and go to bed. At Charlton-on-Otmoor Thomas Trite was rescued from getting lost in the fen by the sound of the church bell and

Bicester lady bell-ringers in 1920. From left to right, front row: Mrs Neal, Mrs Jack Smith, Mrs Wood. Behind them are: Mrs Capewell (a dressmaker), Miss Wood, Miss Jackson, Mrs Harry Jackson, Mrs J. Young.

left money for it to be rung every evening at 8.00 p.m. to help others. This was done until the outbreak of war in 1939. Bells were rung to celebrate the end of the old year and beginning of the new, to celebrate weddings and mark funerals, on special days such as Oak Apple Day and 5 November, to summon women to glean in the fields after harvest, and on Shrove Tuesday.

Some villages have rhymes associated with their bells. The Headington bell asks 'Which Bells ring best?' to which Headington Quarry bells respond 'We do, we do.' Headington says 'Who eats all the bread and cheese?' and Quarry replies 'We two, Quarry hogs.' The Blewbury bell had to be cast three times, hence the rhyme:

> Three times hung and three times cast,
> Blewbury's tenor cast at last.

The churchyard was the site of entertainments until the Reformation, and entries can be found in churchwardens' accounts such as those of Henley-on-Thames and Abingdon of buying bells for the morris men and providing costumes for Robin Hood plays.

In some places people were permitted to walk on the church leads, as at Bloxham where the Revd Harry Davies wrote in 1825, 'It was the custom here formerly when the Church leads were under repair, for the boys and girls to go

Rushes were strewn on Trinity Sunday and the two following Sundays at Shenington, where a piece of ground was left to provide the rushes. Mr Cook, the Parish Clerk whose family carried out the ceremony over several generations, is shown on the left. The photograph was taken by Kenneth Cardus, c. 1967.

up thither and mark the shape and size of their shoes with the sharp point of a knife, inserting the initials of the name and the date of the year in the centre.' Shapes dating back to 1659 have been found at Nether Worton and it was still done in Lower Heyford in the early twentieth century.

A surviving medieval parish ritual is Beating the Bounds at Ascension. It was important to check that the boundaries had not been encroached when there were few maps, as the Church was entitled to a tithe (10 per cent) from each parishioner. The bounds are still beaten in Oxford, with the vicar, choirboys and congregation having to walk through shops such as Marks & Spencer in Queen Street, which forms the boundary of three parishes, climb fences and so on because, although the boundaries have not changed, the topography has. Nowadays instead of beating the choirboys at each mark so that they would remember them, the boys use their peeled willow wands to beat the mark, which is chalked white, shouting 'Mark, mark, mark' as they do so.

In large parishes such as Bampton the beating was done over several days. A vital member of their procession was an unmarried woman who carried a paddle and cut crosses to mark the boundaries. Bread and beer were consumed in the churchyard at the end of each day. Many boundaries were perambulated in 1974, a year of boundary changes, but it is now seldom kept up. In some places, such as Drayton St Leonard, the ceremony was combined with one for blessing the crops.

Choir and parishioners of St Michael-at-the-Northgate parish beating the bounds at Worcester College, Oxford, in 1992. After the ceremony the choristers have a meal at Lincoln College at which they are served specially brewed ivy beer.

four

RITES OF PASSAGE

Birth and Childhood

The phases of life are marked in religion by christening, confirmation, marriage and the last rites of death and burial. People have developed superstitions to encourage good luck at these times and beliefs are universal.

In 1520 a couple from South Leigh, John Phipps and his wife, tried sympathetic magic in their attempt to conceive a child: they were brought up before the churchwardens and accused of idolatry because they kept a baby's cradle next to their bed and treated it as though it contained a child.

Many omens indicated an imminent pregnancy: being the first person visited by a mother and her new baby, particularly if the mother had not been churched (scattering mice, this was referred to in Yarnton); the Balscote belief that one pregnancy in a village will mean two more shortly (there are newspaper articles today about pregnancies in some workplaces coming in clutches) or an apron falling off (perhaps in itself the sign of a thickening waist), as found at Adderbury and Drayton near Abingdon, the latter in the 1970s. At Heyford they said that if new shoes were put on a table, the woman who had done so would have a child within the year. At Headington two crows flying over the house indicated a birth in the family. Seeing a falling star was a sign of a birth in Witney, and at Great Milton a good nutting year foretold plenty of boy babies.

There was an ancient belief that at the time of birth evil spirits abounded, so in primitive societies men sometimes pretended to go through the birth process to distract the attention of the spirits. This theory may be behind the idea of couvade, in which men suffer pains during pregnancy, which also indicated close sympathy between the couple. Some believed that if the man did not suffer the marriage was unhappy. An Oxfordshire woman said in 1936 that a good husband always suffered from toothache and a local man always knew when his wife became pregnant because he had violent toothache.

Some babies are born with a caul, the remains of the foetal sac, on their heads. This was considered extremely lucky: as it protected the baby within the womb, it was a talisman against drowning. Cauls were sought after by sailors – it was effective to own one, even if it was acquired from someone else. In 1954 a Banbury midwife tried to purchase one for £10 for a sailor friend, but the mother kept it for her baby boy.

When mothers gave birth at home, a divination to ascertain how many babies she would have was to throw the afterbirth on the fire and count how often it popped, according to a Witney nurse in 1936.

Birthmarks were thought to be caused by something that had affected the mother during pregnancy. In the Vale of White Horse it was said that if a mother craved port wine, a blackberry or a strawberry, it was important to satisfy the craving quickly, or a mark might appear on the child. The baby should always be taken up before it went down, they said at Spelsbury, even if the nurse only stood on a chair with it.

Birth was a cause for celebration so food was often provided, such as the bread and cheese the Kidlington Overseers of the Poor gave poor families when the wife was 'brought to bed'. It is not clear whether the Rocking Cakes brought to a Gossiping at Wendlebury, to be given to the baby's father, were for a christening or to be served when the baby was born.

Historically, christenings often took place soon after birth as the mortality rate was high, and the child was not considered a full human being before baptism and unbaptised souls would not go to heaven. It was customary for the husband to provide a groaning cake and a large cheese, which was cut in the centre at the baby's birth and gradually hollowed out to form a ring shape large enough to pass the child through on the day of the christening to symbolise rebirth. Often a slice of groaning cake was kept in the house for years. After the christening girls put

Many christening robes such as this early nineteenth century one belonging to the Waine family of Blackthorn and Buckingham, have been passed down over several generations. It used to be said that girls should be christened first or they would develop beards as adults.

groaning cake under their pillows and hoped to dream of their future husbands. Women invited to the christening brought cakes and the first one was presented to the minister. At Over Norton a ring-shaped christening chine was cut from around the pig's neck, cured, and after cooking the slots cut into it were stuffed with sage.

At Shillingford it was believed that babies should not be taken out of the house until they were a month old, and even then the baby's face should be veiled. At one time it was thought dangerous to weigh babies: in 1935 a woman refused to have her baby weighed by the district nurse because an older child had 'gone funny' and she was convinced it was because he had been weighed too often. At Lower Heyford no child under a year old was allowed to see its face in the mirror or have its nails cut (before that the mother should bite them, or the baby would become a thief).

It was customary to give gifts to babies, even to a stranger, often a silver coin, perhaps sympathetic magic to start the child on a road to riches; silver was also thought to have protective qualities.

The mother stayed indoors until purified by the ceremony of churching which recognised her role as a new mother and gave official sanction to a resumption of sexual intercourse. In the sixteenth century many churches had a special seat for new mothers at the back. Churching was commonly performed until the early 1950s, some women not being happy to go out shopping until after the service. It was also thought at Stratton Audley that if one crossed the road before churching, bad luck would follow.

It was unlucky to lose a milk tooth so it had to be burnt. Mollie Harris said that at Ducklington the offending tooth was thrown on the fire and a rhyme chanted:

> Burn, burn blue tooth
> Please God give me a new tooth.

The child was then given a penny by the fairies. If the tooth was lost at school it was taken home to be burnt on the kitchen fire. If a dog swallowed a child's first tooth, it was said at Spelsbury, the new tooth would be a fang. A wide gap between the front teeth indicated generosity, or a voyage around the world.

Courtship and Marriage

In the past country people tended to marry partners who lived nearby, as travel was less extensive than today, which may have made divining who one's future love was to be more feasible. Perhaps, if a girl let it be known that she was thinking of doing a divination, a young man who fancied her might turn up at the appropriate moment. However some divinations seem to have an inexplicable supernatural element.

John Aubrey described a love charm from Albury in *Remaines of Gentilisme and Judaisme*:

A magicall receipt to know whom one shall marry. Egges roasted hard, and the yelke taken out and salt put in its sted, so filled up, to be eaten fasting, without supper, when you go to bed. I thinke only one egge. Mrs. Fines of Albury in Oxfsh. Did this: she dreamt of an ancient grey or white haird man and such a shape which was her husband. This I heard from her owne mouth.

He also mentioned an early form of the dumb cake divination:

> The maids of Oxfordshire have a way of forseeing their sweethearts by making a dumb cake, that is, on some Fryday-night, several Maids and Bachelors bring every one a little flower [i.e. flour] and everyone a little salt, and every one blows an egge. And every one helps to make it into paste, then every one makes ye cake and lays it on the gridiron, and every one breaks a piece and eats one part and laies the other part under their pillow to dream of ye person they shall marry. But all this to be done in serious silence w'hout one word or one smile, or else the cake looses the name and the virtue.

This is the heart of the matter with divinations: by building up anticipation, the divination is more likely to work. In a more recent version of the dumb cake divination the girl would make a dough cake in silence on Christmas Eve, and prick her initials on the cake, then leave the door ajar and wait in silence until the clock struck midnight, when her future husband should walk into the room, prick his initials on the cake next to hers and walk out again without a work being spoken. A Hanborough girl did this and a soldier walked in and pricked his initials on the cake. In passing through the doorway he knocked a fragment off his sword, which she kept. They never mentioned the divination and subsequently married. Years later the woman came across the sword fragment and showed it to her husband, admitting that she had done the divination. He was so angry that he found it hard to forgive her: he had experienced great pains at the time she forced him to appear but had no memory of entering the house.

Three girls from North Leigh crept to the churchyard at midnight one Halloween, armed with hempseed. The first one walked round the churchyard, throwing the hempseed over her shoulder, chanting:

> I sow hempseed,
> Hempseed I sow.
> He that is to be my husband come after me and mow,
> Not in his best or his Sunday array,
> But in the clothes that he wears every day.

She expected the hempseed to magically grow up behind her so that the wraith of her future husband could come behind her and cut it down with his sickle. Although she followed the ritual to the letter, to her disappointment she saw nothing, and died a spinster aged eighty-three. The second girl only got half way through the ritual before she started shrieking in terror. After she had calmed down she admitted that she had seen her own coffin, and she died the next year. The third girl was too afraid to try, and the ritual was subsequently banned in the village.

At Ducklington nuts were placed on the fire at Halloween, named for the girl and her lover; if they burnt together their love would last. Alternatively girls would peel an apple, carefully keeping all the peel in one long piece, and throw it over the shoulder to fall in the initial of the girl's future love.

To find out whether your love was true you could pick four long blades of grass, called Lovelaces, and tie them in four knots, two at each end, saying as you did so:

> If you love me, cling all round me.
> If you hate me, fall off quite.
> If you neither love nor hate
> Come in two at last.

If the grasses formed a ring, the man would be faithful, if the knots fell apart he hated you, if the grasses fell in two pieces he was indifferent. A more light-hearted variant of the cherry stone rhyme was done with a stem of grass called Bennet, beginning at the bottom of the stalk and finishing at the top, taking a seed between the thumb and finger to say each word or sentence, the one finishing with the top seed determining the fortune:

> Whom shall I marry?
> A rich man, a poor man, a beggar man, a farmer, a thief.
> How shall I go to church?
> Coach, carriage, wheelbarrow, chaise.
> What shall I wear?
> Silk, satin, cotton, rags.

Omens could foretell an imminent marriage: two clocks heard striking together, or two spoons accidentally placed in the same saucer, they said at Spelsbury. If a girl stumbled going upstairs she would marry shortly provided that she did not look backwards. If a patchwork quilt was started in a house, the daughters would not marry until it was finished, then one or more would marry within the year. In north Oxfordshire the bridesmaid who caught the bouquet or was the first to reach it would be the first to marry, and the girl to secure the first pin from the bride's dress as she changed to go on honeymoon would marry shortly or be lucky in some other way.

In Filkins around 1930 George Swinford recorded:

A good wife should be like three things and should not be like three things:
1. She should be like a snail to keep within her house; but she should not be like a snail to carry all she has upon her back.
2. She should be like an echo to speak when spoken to, but she should not be like an echo to have always the last word.
3. She should be like a town clock always to keep time and regularity, but she should not be like a town clock to speak so loud that all the town should hear her.

Country people could not always afford a wedding ring, so sometimes in Wychwood Forest the loop of the church key was used as a ring during the ceremony, or a ring would be borrowed. It was unlucky to remove a wedding ring, and particularly so to lose or break it, which foretold the breaking of the marriage or the death of a partner.

May was considered an unlucky month to marry, which possibly dates back to the Roman era when April was sacred to Venus and June to Juno, so to marry in May slighted both goddesses. Also it was the old men's month and the festival of Lemuria during which bathing and wearing cosmetics was forbidden. It was said:

> Marry in Lent,
> Sure to repent

And:

> Who marries between the Sickle and the Scythe
> Will never thrive.

This reflects how busy the agricultural year was between the hay and wheat harvests, hence a bad time for country people to wed.

The bride often borrowed a veil from a happily married woman to bring herself good luck, but the veil should never be tried on at the same time as the dress, as to see one's complete outfit in the mirror before the day of the wedding was to tempt fate.

Except among the wealthy, the bride walked in procession to the church. Children at Iffley and elsewhere strewed rose petals before the bride (reflecting

Sometimes triumphal arches are provided as the bride and groom leave church. Here the Headington Morris Men made an arch with sticks used in their dances, for John Warland and Beryl Pitt at Headington Quarry church in 1950. The morris men are, from left to right: Arthur Kimber, Charlie Jones, Jim Phillips, Harry and William Kimber.

A magnificently decorated wedding cake made by William Edmund Smith and his son Morley at their bakery at No. 23 Sheep Street, Bicester, c. 1912.

the Tudor practice of strewing sweet-smelling herbs such as rosemary and evergreens in the street to protect against mud and give a sweeter perfume to smelly streets), and were rewarded with a slice of wedding cake. The bride always left home via the front door, and hoped that en route a black cat would approach her, or that she would see a dirty chimney sweep, especially if he offered her a small gift (perhaps because soot indicated fertility). The last thing she wanted to meet was a funeral party.

If the marriage was unhappy, and the husband was known to beat his wife, villagers showed their disapproval by playing rough music to shame the wrong-doer, which was performed as late as the 1930s in Eynsham. At Shotover villagers processed round Stanton St John, Holton and Forest Hill en route to the man's cottage where they banged old tins, made speeches about his cruelty and burnt an effigy of him. At South Stoke rough music was accompanied by a song:

> There is a man in our town
> Who often beats his wife,
> So if he does it any more,
> We'll put his nose right out before.
> Holler boys, holler boys,
> Make the bells ring,
> Holler boys, holler boys.
> God save the King.

At Chipping Norton it was called skimmetting, and wheat husks were thrown outside the miscreant's door to indicate that thrashing had been done there. Sometimes the woman was at fault, as at Coombe in the 1930s when people paraded without an effigy and called out the woman's name and offence.

Until the twentieth century it was impossible to get a divorce unless one was rich, and even then divorcees were ostracised from polite society, so wife selling was an unorthodox – and not strictly legal – way of changing partners. The *Oxford Journal* recorded wife selling in Oxford on 5 August 1876:

> One Broom of Kennington near this city sold his wife to a person of the name of Pantin, of Little London, for five shillings to whom she was publicly delivered after with a halter about her neck; but it seems that Pantin was very soon sick of his bargain, for in the afternoon of the same day, he generously made a present of her to Sadler, the Woodward of Bagley.

Three years later, on 12 December, the paper recorded that a navvy working on the Oxford canal went to the market place where he 'tied a penny slip round the waist of his wife, the end of which he held fast till he had pocketed three shillings in part payment, the purchaser not abounding in cash; he then put the cord into the hands of the new husband and took French leave. The woman immediately called for her second wedding ring, which being put on, she eagerly kissed the fellow, with whom she walked off.'

An old man from Hanborough took his wife to Witney market where he sold her for £5. Around 1855 a Burford man sold his wife to a man who lived in Simon Wisdom's House. The outraged townsfolk played rough music outside the house with horns, tin whistles, trumpets, tins and sticks, and burnt the purchaser in effigy. He ran out armed with a pitchfork, grabbed the effigy and dropped it into the River Windrush, then sold the wife back to her original husband for £15. What the wife had to say about it is not recorded.

Death and Burial

Death has always been a part of life, but now more people die in hospital and death is dealt with by undertakers rather than laying out the corpse and keeping the body in the house until the funeral, so elaborate death rites have disappeared.

As late as 2 January 1909 the *Oxford Times* recorded a death divination which took place on St Mark's Eve in North Oxfordshire. Young people gathered in the churchyard as the church clock struck 11 p.m. and remained silent until the clock struck one, expecting to see a procession of all the people who would die in the coming year. Freeland children often ran round the church eleven times, but never twelve, as that foretold death within the year.

There were numerous omens of death: if a corpse did not 'set' there would be another death within twelve months (at Leafield), crocks rattling, a spider making a ticking noise, two black crows on a line, a knock on the door with no-one there, crickets rapidly leaving a house, a dog howling, the clock striking twelve during the second sermon or hymn (at Adderbury), the fire burning with a bright hole in the middle (at Stoke Row), a coffin shape formed in ironed linen or a loaf of bread and a candle guttering and the grease spiralling to form a 'winding sheet'. It was taboo to wash clothes on Good Friday or New Year's Day or to wash blankets in May, or seat thirteen people at a table. People dreaded a picture falling from the wall for no apparent reason, scissors falling point downwards, or a glass ringing (indicating the death of a sailor). Dressmakers avoided accidentally stitching a hair into their work. It was bad if the eyes of the corpse remained open, or the corpse stayed in the house over a Sunday, or the funeral had to be postponed. People encountering a funeral procession would walk a little way with it to avert bad luck.

Plant omens of death included flowers with drooping heads, such as snowdrops, which should not be brought into the house, dead flowers found outside picked up, red and white flowers in a vase (especially in hospitals where they were described as 'blood and bandages'), flowers blooming out of season, fruit trees blossoming twice in one year or out of season, lilac brought in, parsley transplanted or given away and red hot pokers blooming twice.

Many omens were associated with birds: coming into the house, tapping on the window, flying into a closed window or flying down a chimney, cocks crowing at midnight, carrion crows or owls perching near the house and a robin perching on a chair.

The son of a Minster Lovell family emigrated to America and when their clock, which had been silent for years, suddenly struck one the mother immediately knew her son was dead, and so it transpired.

Occasionally people see visions of the dead at the moment of death: G.H. Powell in *Stonesfield through the Ages* told a story about Vic Davies, who as a boy lived in Well Lane. His grandfather slept in the attic, reached by a staircase from Vic's room. Vic told his mother at breakfast that he had seen his grandfather come down the stairs during the night carrying a lit candle, but the grandfather had been taken to the Woodstock Workhouse Infirmary a few days before. It transpired that the old man had died during the night.

R.E. Moreau wrote in *The Departed Village* about a shepherd's wife in Roke on her deathbed. A neighbour went in at five o'clock one morning and the shepherd called to her to enter. As she lifted the latch a figure in white, resembling the shepherd's wife as she looked when healthy, turned to her and smiled. A few minutes later the shepherd's wife died and the neighbour identified the figure as her spirit which had come for her.

A way to ease a person into death after a long struggle, in the Vale of White Horse, was to wrap the dying person in a still warm sheepskin taken from a newly killed sheep. Shepherds were buried with their crooks and a piece of wool to explain to God why they were seldom in church and some were buried in their wedding smocks. Some women put aside a wedding dress, a white dress or nightdress for burial and a linen handkerchief to be placed over the face; one woman prepared a nightdress, pillowcase, sheets and pins for her funeral. Women at North Leigh were buried in white stockings instead of their everyday black ones. In 1938 a child who died in the Radcliffe Infirmary was dressed by her mother in her best clothes and a new woollen coat to 'keep her warm'. Wedding sheets were often reused as winding sheets. One woman in the village took responsibility for washing corpses and dressing them in their burial clothes. At North Leigh the coffin was lined with a wreath of every herb growing in the garden except thyme.

At Shipton-under-Wychwood the corpse was measured for the coffin using a piece of string: three knots were tied to indicate the length, width at the shoulders and the width of the hips. It was important to protect the corpse until the soul had time to pass to the other world: mirrors were covered to prevent the soul being trapped by seeing itself, windows were opened so it could escape freely and the corpse should never be locked in – in fact the house door should remain open until the corpse had been carried out of sight, they said at Headington Quarry. Sometimes green turf wrapped in paper was placed by the dead man's leg, salt was put on the chest and a candle kept alight in the room. The eyes were fixed shut, sometimes with coins, as anyone who came within the dead man's sight was doomed to follow him. The coins also indicated the fee to be rowed to the other world. Sometimes the feet were tied together to prevent the Devil from entering the body. Many people felt that the corpse should not be left alone.

Church bells were rung to announce a death. At Somerton this was done as soon as a death occurred at one time, but by the early twentieth century only between sunrise and sunset as was more customary elsewhere. In Adderbury some families claimed the privilege of having the tenor bell rung to announce a death: four strokes announced a man and three a woman and the Invitation Bell was rung for two hours before a funeral. At Banbury the large bell was rung for a time, then five times for a man, four for a woman, three for a boy and two for a girl, known as the Parting Bell. At Lower Heyford and Shipton-under-Wychwood the corpse was chimed into the churchyard.

At the Oxford colleges the death of a member entitled to a coat of arms was signified by depicting his shield against the black-painted canvas background of the hatchment. If he left a widow entitled to arms, her arms, on a white background, were impaled with his; alternatively his college arms could be used, again on a white background.

It has recently become customary to leave bunches of flowers at the site of a fatal accident which echoes a custom of cutting cross shapes in stone or turf at the site of a death. There is a cross on the stone gatepost at The Priory, Iffley, which commemorated the death of an undergraduate who was thrown from his horse, and another above the choir seats in the church, supposedly marking the death of a workman.

Many coffins were carried in walking funerals from the house to the church. There was a common superstition that if a coffin was carried over private land it created a right of way. This led to problems for P.A.V. Gunnington, who controlled the toll gate at Iffley on behalf of Lincoln College, when Frederick Penfold drowned in the lock in 1948. The police offered to pay the fee to take the body through the toll gate, but Mr Gunnington refused to let them pass and made them carry the body over the wall and across private land, fearing that if he let them through the right to charge a toll ceased. He was severely censured for this by the coroner.

At Brightwell Baldwin a woman who had recently moved to the village saw people wandering through her private wood, picking snowdrops, and when she remonstrated with them they claimed that there was a right of way as the previous year the Squire had died during snowy weather and his coffin had to be carried through the wood, creating a perpetual right of way. At Waterstock when a funeral procession had to go through Miss Ashfield's land because of bad weather, to avoid creating a right of way, each gate across the land was locked and the procession halted at each gate while the key was collected from the house, then the gate was locked after them.

In the seventeenth century mourners at more wealthy funerals such as that of Edward, the elder brother of Anthony Wood, were presented with gloves, wine and biscuits. Traveller Conrad von Uffenbach described an Oxford funeral in 1710:

> The coffin, over which was spread a large black velvet pall, stood on two chairs before the door of a house. When the time came to make a move, some wretched fellows in coloured clothing crept under the cloth and took the coffin on their shoulders without a bier. About eight respectable townsfolk (who … were not in black) seized the corners of the velvet pall and carried them, and after them followed about eight couples of mourners or relatives, male and female, who walked in two and two leaving the others to follow in a crowd… They all marched along in colours and every one had a stick of rosemary in one hand and in the other a white roll of paper containing white gloves. The house of mourning provides both of these – a great expense as the poorest quality cost at least one shilling and sixpence. Distinguished people are buried by torchlight.

Only the principal mourners and relatives wore black.

Special arrangements were made for children's funerals. At Long Hanborough when a baby died in the late nineteenth century four young women dressed in white, wearing white bonnets tied under the chin, carried the coffin which was placed on a white cloth tied up at the four corners. At Iffley four girls carried a white or pale blue coffin, supported by white ribbons threaded through the handles. Children carried the coffin at North Aston and Somerton and at Steeple Aston boys carried coffins for dead boys, and girls coffins for dead girls. At North Leigh coffins of young people were carried by four young men wearing black coats, white trousers and white gloves, while girls acted as pall-bearers, wearing white dresses and gloves with black jackets and straw hats covered with white muslin.

In mid-nineteenth-century Oxford the bellman often preceded funerals of undergraduates to college chapels or to St Mary's church in the High Street, possibly to summon friends to the funeral.

Walking funerals for the poor at Iffley were led by the coffin, carried by four bearers, paid two shillings each for their duties, followed by mourners carrying posies of home-grown flowers, while the passing bell was tolled. Those who could afford it dressed in black crêpe, and sometimes artificial wreaths in glass cases were purchased by the better off.

At Piddington the church provided smocks for the pall-bearers, so that they could come to the funeral straight from their work. As these wore out one of them was copied and a set of six new ones made, worn with black hats and gloves. The first funeral at which these smocks were not used was in 1950, for the funeral of the woman who had organised for them to be made, probably because she was the one who went round and collected them for a funeral. The smocks are now in the Oxfordshire Museum collection. Apparently many villages once had smocks for pall-bearers.

When a waterman was buried in Oxford in 1850 three watermen walked either side of his hearse wearing blue jackets and white trousers, followed by the chief mourners, family and friends with a procession of watermen in deep mourning walking in pairs bringing up the rear.

Jackson's *Oxford Journal* of 28 July 1849 recorded the death of sixteen-year-old Fanny Bossom, a laundress' daughter who died of consumption. She was laid in her coffin with her arms across her breast and a cross of nails at the head and foot of the coffin, which was carried from Fish Row to St Thomas's church, where: '… it was joined by the children of the school, who preceded the bier, and scattered flowers along the way, while a large attendance of choristers and singing men chanted the service, as well as at the grave. On the conclusion of the service the mourners and many others re-entered the church and partook of the holy sacrament.'

Gypsies have elaborate funeral rites. Harriet Bowers died in 1953 aged sixty-eight at Garsington. On the morning of the funeral her coffin was carried out of her caravan, where it had rested overnight accompanied by a lighted candle at her head, and a sprig of flowers placed on her body. The 300 or so mourners who had travelled from as far as Devon, Somerset and Dorset filed by and kissed her, or touched her lips with their hands. Wreaths were hung from cart wheels before being transferred to the hearse. The women purchased second hand black clothes for the occasion and many had black bands round their heads and the men wore dark clothes. The funeral ceremony was held at the Abingdon cemetery chapel where Mrs Bowers was buried, then mourners returned to Mrs Bowers' caravan at Garsington. Crockery was removed and broken, and all her possessions, including family photographs, were piled up inside the caravan and soaked in paraffin by her youngest son, William, aged twenty-eight. Then the caravan's shafts were removed and placed upright against the door and another relative, Sam Isaacs, set fire to the van which the men pushed over on to its side. Despite the pleas of the RSPCA her two horses were shot, following traditional gypsy rites. The framework of the caravan was later buried. In 1976 Mrs Matilda Smith, a gypsy, died in hospital. Her caravan was taken from Sandford-on-Thames to the local sewage works to be burnt safely.

Sometimes coffins were carried a long way from outlying houses to the church: in the early eighteenth century the coffin of Mr Eldridge, who died near Ramsden, was carried through Wychwood Forest. The bearers put the coffin down to take a break but were distracted into hunting a squirrel, which led them a merry dance until dusk. A sudden snowstorm changed the landmarks and it took the men three days to find the coffin.

Suicides were seldom buried in churchyards, but an exception was made for a butler who had got a girl pregnant at Shipton-under-Wychwood, but apparently blue lights were seen on his grave for many months. About 1803 a harness maker, who sold base metal as silver, committed suicide at the then crossroads where the current Donnington Bridge Road meets the road from Iffley to Oxford when his perfidy was discovered. He was buried in the middle of the road and a skeleton was found there during drainage works in 1895.

People sometimes requested to be buried in strange ways. At Kingham there is a tradition that a man who feared being buried underground was buried within the north wall of the chancel, while at Stanton Harcourt Sir John Harcourt who died in 1330 is supposedly buried upright in the north transept, commemorated by a circular stone in the pavement with a shield bearing his coat of arms. At Old Headington it is said that a soldier requested to be buried standing to attention and was buried upright.

Some people feared being buried alive: Sophia Wykeham, Lady Wenman, who vainly hoped to marry the Duke of Clarence, died in 1870 aged eighty at Thame Park. She apparently instructed that she should lie in the family crypt in an open coffin for seven days after her death, have a dome with a breathing hole incorporated on top of the coffin to contain her coronet and remain above ground for fifty years. Thame Park changed hands and the new owners wanted to restore the chapel so in 1983 the crypt was opened and it was discovered that there was no breathing hole (and no formal instructions about her burial in her will), and that Lady Wenman had merely desired to lie in state. Her coffin and coronet were later buried in the family graveyard at a special committal service, led by the Right Reverend Richard Watson, with about twenty-five guests including Sir Frank and Lady Bowden, former owners of the Park, and neighbour Robin Gibb of the Bee Gees.

There is a possible relic of sin-eating from Ambrosden. It used to be customary for a man to eat bread and ale provided for him, together with a fee, in order to take on the sins of the dead person. At Ambrosden a flagon of ale and a cake were brought by the Minister to the church porch after the burial. A funeral feast was often provided and one man from North Leigh complained that he smelt the ham for his funeral being cooked before he had actually died!

five

THE WORLD OF WORK

Farming Lore

M̲ost people spend the majority of their lives working, and their prosperity is dependent on the success of their work. Superstitions abound to make work more successful, and customs arise to add a sparkle to everyday life.

Until the late nineteenth century the majority of workers in Oxfordshire were agricultural labourers, whose work changed little over centuries until machines appeared in the harvest fields in the late Victorian era and gradually took over much of their work

The agricultural year began at the end of the twelve days of Christmas with Plough Sunday, the Sunday after 6 January, when a plough was taken into church to be ritually blessed and symbolically bring good luck for the year's cultivation. Plough Sunday services were revived at Aston Rowant in 1951 and at Coombe in 1954. The following day, Plough Monday, plough boys got up at dawn and tried to reach the farmhouse hearth before the maidservant could light the fire and boil the kettle. If they succeeded their prize was a cock for their next feast. Then they proceeded round the village, dressed up and with blackened faces, threatening to plough up front lawns if they were not offered money. At Asthall in the late nineteenth century ploughmen shouted:

> Rain, hail or shine,
> The best cock in the yard's mine.

They expected the mistress of the house to bring them a quart of beer with toast floating in it and if it did not appear they pretended to hunt her cocks until it did, a practice called 'winding the cock'. The rhyme at nearby Minster Lovell was nearly the same, but the first line ran:

> Hail, rain, snow or shine…

The agricultural year was regulated to an extent by the ecclesiastical calendar which provided landmarks for such jobs as planting beans at Candlemas (2 February) and potatoes on Good Friday because that day the Devil had no power over the soil (although some said it was only lucky if you had been to church first and others that it was an unlucky day). Beans were planted on 1 or 2 March, definitely before 15 March:

> Sow your beans on David and Chad
> If the weather be good or the weather be bad;
> And if you don't sow them before Benedick
> You had better, I ween, keep them all in the rick.

J.R. Wodhams recorded this in *The Midland Garner* (1884), adding:

> Four beans to sow, when you make your row,
> One to rot, one to grow, one for the pigeon,
>   one for the crow.

Kidney beans were planted on 12 May, Stow-on-the-Wold Fair day, at Filkins, and spring cabbages on Lechlade Fair day (9 September), wheat on Banbury Michaelmas Fair day in Bicester. Planting barley was reckoned by the growth of elm leaves at Forest Hill:

> When the elmen leaf is as big as a mouse's ear,
> Then to sow barley never fear.
> When the elmen leaf is as big as an ox's eye,
> Then say I 'I hie, boys, hie'.

Some places had meadows over which several people held rights, known as Lot Meadows. At Yarnton an elaborate ritual was used to assign areas for mowing: an auction of rights was held at The Grapes public house at Yarnton on St Peter's Day (29 June), then areas for each purchaser were assigned using a set of wooden balls known as mead balls. Strips were marked out with wooden pegs, while the tydals (areas owned by the rectories of Yarnton and Begbroke, so not part of the lot drawing), were differentiated by being marked with stones. As each strip was drawn, it was marked with the initials of the owner and men shuffled their feet to define the edges. The strips used to be cut in one day, but this involved hiring Irish labourers, whose drunkenness led to disorderly behaviour and even untimely death, so the mowing time was extended. After mowing, morris dancing, shows, races and a feast were organised. Afterwards cattle grazed in the meadows. Similar festivities were held at Revel-mede at Bicester, and candle auctions were held to allocate lots at Combe and Bicester.

Port Meadow in Oxford has horses and cattle grazing on it, which are rounded up without warning one day over the summer by the Sheriff of Oxford (as representative of the owners, the Freemen of Oxford), who impounds them at Godstow nunnery until a fine is paid. Round-up methods vary: one Sheriff used a helicopter.

Many farmers, as at Waterperry, refused to begin harvest on a Friday, an unlucky day for new ventures. At Tadmarton and Swalcliffe church bells tolled morning and evening during harvest to tell labourers when to start and finish. Often the whole family worked in the field, the children twisting straw into bands to tie the sheaves, the men reaping and the women making up the sheaves. In some areas such as

Each of the wooden balls used to designate areas to be mown in the Yarnton Lot Meadows is marked with a name: Boat, Boulton, Dunn, Freeman, Gilbert, Green, Harry, Perry, Rothe, Walter Jeoffrey, Waterey Molly, White and William of Bladon, perhaps reflecting names of previous owners or characteristics of the fields. Each ball represents the amount a man can mow in a day.

Haymaking at Frogley's Farm, Bicester. According to Joshua Lamb, writing about Sibford in the *Banbury Guardian* in 1931, the most proficient labourer was made leader and the mowers' song included the words: 'Eat before you're hungry, drink before you're dry, whet your scythe before it rusts and you'll mow as well as I.'

Cottisford a Lord of the Harvest was chosen to regulate the men's work and negoti-
ate a special contract with the farmer. Flora Thompson described one Lord in *Lark
Rise to Candleford*, as an ex-soldier who had a tanned skin, 'darkened by fiercer than
English suns', who wore a wide rush-plaited hat with poppy and bindweed trails.

At Culham when a harvester was unable to keep up with his fellows, particularly if
he was regarded as lazy, his fellows commented that 'He's got the Little White Dog'.

The last sheaf cut was thought to represent the Corn Spirit, so it was often
made into a particularly fine sheaf, sometimes attired in women's dress, and carried back to the farmyard with the last load in great solemnity. At Ducklington,
when the last load was ready to be taken back to the farmyard, boxes containing
women's dresses and finery for the horses were sent down to the field and four
young men dressed up as women then sat in couples on the four horses drawing
the load. The farmer was bedridden in a downstairs room, so the wagon stopped
three times outside his window so that he could see everything. At Bicester the
men shouted 'Harvest Home' as the last load was carried back and threw pails of
water at them in the early nineteenth century. Often a gallon of beer would be
provided to greet the last load back.

At Cottisford, Flora Thompson recorded the song sung as the wagons returned
to the farm with the last load:

> Harvest home! Harvest home!
> Merry, merry, merry harvest home!
> Our bottles are empty, our barrels won't run,
> And we think it's a very dry harvest home.

At Long Hanborough they sang:

> Hip, hip, hip, harvest home!
> A good plum pudding and a bacon bone,
> And that's a very good harvest home.

After the last load had been taken back women were allowed to glean any corn
stalks remaining in the fields, which could provide them with enough flour to
last the winter. At Rotherfield Greys all available types of corn were collected and
made into a 'luck sheaf' which was hung on the farmhouse wall to ensure good
luck and plenty all year. The special sheaf made for the last load was kept in the
farmhouse kitchen or barn throughout the winter and ploughed back into the
soil with the spring sowing, to ensure that the spirit of fertility remained on the
farm. This is the origin of the corn dolly.

Most farmers gave their labourers harvest home suppers of roast beef, Yorkshire
puddings, roast potatoes and plum puddings with lots to eat and drink. Some
songs suggested that if the labourer spilt so much as a drop of his ale the farmer
would expect him to have another glass, as in this song recorded by Angelina
Parker from Long Hanborough:

> Here's a health unto our master,
> The founder of the feast.
> I pray to God with all my heart,

His soul in heaven may rest;
And that ev'rythink may prosper,
Whatever he takes in hand;
For we are all his servants,
And all at his command.
Then drink, boys, drink,
And see that you do not spill;
For if you do, you shall drink two,
For 'tis our master's will.
Here's a health unto our misteris,
The best in one and twenty.
Highho! Is it so, is it so!
Fill him up a little fuller,
For methinks he seems but empty,
And down let him go, let him go, let him go.
And if he drinks too deep
He can go to bed and sleep,
And drive away dull sorrow, care and woe.

Another harvest home song suggests older origins:

Oliver Cromwell is in his grave,
Um, ah, dead in his grave.
There grows a green apple tree over his head,
Un ah, over his head.
The bridle and saddle are laid on the shelf,
Um, ah, laid on the shelf.
If you want any more you may sing it yourself,
Um, ah, sing it yourself.

After harvest home suppers declined, the parish sometimes took over the role, as at Grafton near Clanfield where two marquees were set up in a paddock, one for the children. Food included meat and pastries with jelly and custard for the children. The event started with prayers from the vicar, followed by a real 'blow-out', with much of the children's jelly flying through the air. After the food folk songs such as 'The Farmer's Boy' and 'The Grandfather Clock' were sung, recitations were performed and a broomstick dance done.

Church harvest festivals date from the late nineteenth century. Often a sheaf-shaped loaf was displayed in the church and Mollie Harris remembered that at Ducklington in the early twentieth century the church was packed with people admiring the display of stooks of wheat, enormous marrows, masses of fruit and vegetables, Michaelmas daisies and dahlias.

Other aspects of farming abounded in custom and superstition. Villagers preferred to keep male pigs, believing that if they killed a female pig while she was on heat the meat would become sour. It was unlucky to kill a pig when the moon was waning because that would cause the meat to shrivel in the pan.

Ardley shepherds were pleased if a black lamb was among the first to be born as that indicated a good flock. At Banbury it was bad luck if the first lamb seen in spring was facing you. In Tackley they believed that when the lambs first frolicked rain was near. Shepherds were given pancakes when the first lamb was born; at Charlton-on-Otmoor if the first lambs were twins, he had sugar on both sides. Shipton-under-Wychwood shepherds docked their lambs' tails when the moon was waning, fearing that otherwise the lambs would die. The shepherd was given the tails and made them into a pie.

Sheep shearing was a busy time: often several farmers gathered their sheep together to form a 'shearing club'. On the last day of shearing boiled leg of mutton, plum pudding and alcohol were served at a feast at Sibford, according to Joshua Lamb. At Chilsworth men wore posies on their hats and coats at sheep shearing and feasted afterwards.

Horsemen or carters worked longer hours on the farm than other labourers. At Berrick Salome, which was probably typical, they fed the horses at 5 a.m., then went home for breakfast, returning at 7 a.m., taking a break for lunch while the horses munched the contents of their nosebags, and ate dinner between 3 p.m. and 4 p.m., returning afterwards to groom the horses, give them a snack and bed them down for the night. Horsemen received slightly more pay in compensation and were highly regarded.

At seed-sowing carters were given seed cake and sometimes suppers were held – at Asthal plum puddings, meat, cabbage and beer were on the menu. If a young horseman misbehaved he was punished in the Vale of White Horse, according to Alfred Williams, by being thrown over a horse on to the ground. By a judicious use of herbs, which stimulated the horse's sensitive sense of smell, the

The Hutchins family shearing in 1930. On the far right is Frederick Hutchins (1877-1955) who was champion sheep shearer for Oxfordshire and Berkshire and sheared 60,314 sheep between 1911 and 1929. The other shearers include Charles Hutchins, Frederick's son William Henry Hutchins, and William George Hutchins. During shearing they slept in barns, leaving home early on Monday mornings and returning home late on Saturday.

horseman could exert influence over the powerful beasts. At Islip mandrake was grated into feed to encourage a horse's appetite, while deadly nightshade was used at Stonesfield as a drenching medicine. At Freeland if a mare was liable to miscarriage a black donkey or a goat would be put in the field with her.

Horsemen were enormously proud of their brasses and bells which were thought to avert the Evil Eye, the bells having a secondary purpose of warning other vehicles that something was coming along a winding lane. Millers' wagons were drawn by four or five horses with bells on their collars; in Oxford the children would shout after them:

> Bell horses, bell horses,
> What time of day?
> One o'clock, two o'clock,
> Three and away.

Horseshoes, which were considered lucky, were always hung with the tips upwards, except by the blacksmith, in case the 'good luck' ran out. They were often hung on doors or outside a house. Human shoes were connected to horses at Hanwell:

> A shoe on the table
> A horse dead in the stable.

The Watercress Queen

Ewelme was famous for the watercress grown there, much of which was sent to London. The workers sang as they toiled:

> While strolling out one evening
> Down by the running stream,
> Where water lilies were growing,
> It was a lovely scene.
> The sight I saw was better,
> A Damsel like a Queen,
> She was gathering watercress
> Down by the old mill stream.
> Her hair hung down in tresses
> As gently flowed the stream.
> She was gathering watercresses
> Was that fair Watercress Queen.
> I asked if she was lonely.
> She answered with a smile,
> 'Oh Sir, I am not lonely
> For this is my daily toil.
> I have to be up so early
> To gather my cresses green.'
> She told me her name was …
> Better known as the Watercress Queen.

Telling the Bees

Bees were kept to supplement the family income and to provide honey for the household. It was important to build up a rapport with them, as they were easily alarmed, but if they became used to the voice of their keeper they were calmed, so bees were told about important events. A Headington woman neglected to tell the bees when her mother died and lost two hives. At Kencot when someone in the house died, the oldest occupant must walk three times round each hive and repeat distinctly three times the full name of the dead person, or the bees would leave.

Flora Thompson wrote in *A Country Calendar* that when a girl became engaged the beekeeper should say to the bees:

> Bees, bees, there's joy in the house,
> For a maid has promised to wed!

Sometimes hives were decorated with wedding favours, and at a death with black crêpe. In the Vale of White Horse Alfred Williams said that bees were informed of the death of the Squire and the King. If a swarm settled on dry wood it was an omen of death. When bees swarmed they were tanged or rung home – at Blackthorn this was done by beating a fire shovel with a door key. It was believed that if the ringing was not done the bees could not be reclaimed if they settled in another person's land.

Builders' Lore

Building could be a hazardous occupation: it was said in Charlbury in around 1880 that workmen would say when they began a big project: 'Ah, there'll be one or two killed on that job – jest to bind it together like.'

Builders were sometimes treated to refreshment – at St Michael's church, Oxford, in 1954 workmen doing restoration after a fire were given bread, cheese and beer by the vicar, Canon R.R. Martin, following a tradition recorded in the church's accounts over the centuries. The builders had representatives at the service when the church re-opened.

In the same year at Islip the custom of 'wetting the chimney' or 'capping out' was revived at Mr G.W. Taylor's new house: when the final chimney block was laid workers hoisted a Union Jack to announce the 'wetting'. If drink had not been forthcoming they would have placed a tile over the chimney and hoisted a black flag instead. To complete the ceremony Mr Taylor climbed the scaffolding to pour ale down the chimney.

Witney blankets

The woollen trade was important in the Cotswolds, which stretch into the western fringes of Oxfordshire. Dr Plot commented in *Natural History of Oxfordshire* (1677) that St Blaise's Day, 3 February, was celebrated in Oxfordshire:

When countrywomen went about and made good cheer, and if they found any of their Neighbour-women a Spinning set their Distaff on fire.

Witney firms specialised in making blankets, exporting them all over the world until the business collapsed in the 1990s. Witney quill winders brought their quill sticks to the mill-owners on Shrove Tuesday and were granted a feast of pancakes and ale. The Tuckers or Finishers had feasts in May and November, when the Masters paid the Tuckers, which was changed to one Shrove Tuesday feast. At the May feast there were entertainments such as cricket and skittles and after the meal men were given one clay pipe for each year they had attended the feast. A song entitled *Wonderfully Curious*, composed around the time of the Battle of Waterloo, was sung, which began:

> The wondrous globe on which we live
> Is quite surrounded everywhere
> With something quite invisible
> It's called the atmospheric air.
> The air is fluid light and thin,
> Which forms of gas it does combine;
> It carries sound in order well
> When put in motion it is wind.
> Chorus: O! how curious, wonderfully curious,
> The laws of nature are indeed
> Most wonderfully curious.

A handloom weaver at Early's blanket-making factory in Witney, c. 1900. The family firm existed for over 300 years, closing in the 1990s.

Village Craftsmen

The blacksmith was one of the most respected craftsmen, his manipulation of iron being considered almost magical. His pride in his work is reflected in this epitaph from Spelsbury:

> My sledge and hammer lies declined,
> My bellows too have lost their wind,
> My fire's extinct, my coal's decayed,
> And in the dust my vice is laid:
> My anvil's mute, my course is run,
> My nails are drove, my work is done.

A group of blacksmiths led by Fred Smith about to fire volleys on four anvils in Bicester Market Square to celebrate Queen Victoria's Diamond Jubilee in 1897.

Alfred Williams recorded a folksong about the cobbler in *Folk Songs of the Upper Thames*:

> He's cutting and contriving,
> Hammer, nails and driving,
> Hemp, wax and leather;
> Madam, if you please
> To pay me your fees,
> It's fourpence ha'penny all together.

The Printing Industry

Oxford has been a major centre for printing and publishing since the middle ages, although changes in technology have seen the end of traditional printing methods. At Oxford University Press, according to Mike Belsen in *On the Press*, apprentices were victims of tricks such as being sent on fools' errands for striped ink or italic spaces. In the machine room boys planted stink bombs under the brake pedals of machines or surreptitiously put slices of composition rolls in sandwiches in place of meat.

When their apprenticeship finished budding journeymen were 'banged out', running the gauntlet of their fellow workers, who made lots of noise as they went to the printer's office to collect their indentures. Sometimes the apprentice was put into a trolley and paraded round the Press and into the Quad, pursued by crowds banging chases with metal side-sticks, while machine minders and bindery men were covered with ink and glue in unmentionable places.

The end of indentures was marked by the apprentice entertaining his fellows for a feast, which could be as simple as bread, cheese and beer, or rise to a dinner in a private room at Jericho House. At the latter a loving cup of punch was passed round and a toast made:

> Here's to him who now is free,
> Who once was apprentice bound:
> We'll drink his health and merry, merry be,
> We'll drink his health all round.

Young apprentices were well cared for, with the opportunity to attend night school. On Good Friday they were given two hot-cross buns, and at Christmas two mince pies.

six

HEARTH AND HOME

Objects Hidden in Buildings

Home is where people should feel safe and secure. This is reflected in many superstitions, and especially by the objects buried in buildings, sometimes when they were built, presumably to propitiate any 'earth spirits' that might be disturbed by building, or when major repairs such as a new roof were undertaken, and perhaps to provide some sort of guardian to ward off evil. When the seventeenth-century Globe Room panelling was removed from the Reindeer Inn in Parsons Street, Banbury, the dried out body of a cat was found behind it, but it is not clear whether it was placed there or trapped during building. Two kittens which had died of natural causes were discovered in a central heating duct under the dining room floor of a Wheatley house which was installed in the 1930s. One of the skeletons was inadvertently removed by the builders, but the second was reburied in the house.

Stoneware 'Bellarmine' bottle, dating from between 1650 and 1700, decorated with a rosette and the face of Cardinal Bellarmine, found under the floor of No. 36 Market Square, Bicester, when the strong rooms of Barclays Bank were extended in 1960. It may have been put there for protective purposes or more specifically as protection against witchcraft.

During the Middle Ages pottery was often buried in foundations. An enormous vessel, probably for brewing ale, 55cm high dating from around the late twelfth or thirteenth century, was found 45cm below the modern ground level covered with two pieces of flat stone while digging foundations for a new building at Churchill. It contained an iron key, two links of iron chain and a rolled up piece of lead. Iron was thought to protect against evil. Nearby were scattered pottery sherds of various dates and a coin of Edward III. A bowl was buried in the chancel of the church at Woodperry which may have been a foundation sacrifice. A group of Baluster jugs (one containing a coin of Henry III) and small pottery bottles was found in 1838 buried near the wall of Trinity College garden in Oxford, probably deposited around 1290 when the boundary wall of Durham College, the precursor of Trinity, was constructed.

When the Bodleian Library was extended two green glazed pitchers were found three feet deep beneath the chimney stack of No. 47 Broad Street, probably connected with a medieval house on the site. At Weston on the Green an almost complete bottle containing a white compacted substance was found under the kitchen floor of a sixteenth-century house and several coins were hidden under the sitting room floor and medieval pottery by the fireplace.

Until the late nineteenth century there is much evidence of such protective magical practices. Roofs were protected because of the danger of fire, and chimneys were thought to give access to evil spirits so protective items were placed in chimneys, behind the recesses of first floor fireplaces, between roof and ceiling and under attic floors.

Shoes were often chosen for this purpose, perhaps because of their intimate association with their wearers they were considered lucky, were associated with fertility and were a suitable shape to trap evil spirits. Sometimes new shoes were buried, but more commonly they were well used, occasionally deliberately damaged. A worn boy's boot with a damaged heel dating from around 1850 was found under the rafters at No. 6 Spring Street, Chipping Norton, with straw and sherds of a broken pottery jug with a pale blue pattern around it. Boots were bricked up in a cottage in Lidstone.

Sometimes other objects are found: a leather hat was found in the roof space of the seventeenth-century Potters Folly at Horspath and a doll with a glazed china head and blonde hair in a crinoline dress with a straw-stuffed skirt, probably designed as a decorative pincushion, was found under the bedroom floor at Lower Farm, Elsfield. At Wantage a collection of nineteenth-century items was found in a wattle and daub wall by the fireplace in the top floor of the Falcon Inn: a fragment of a pancheon, a top hat, a pumice stone, leather, six sherds of pottery and nine bones from butchered joints. A hoard found at Thame appeared to have been deposited over a century and included a felt hat, part of a christening robe, broken lace bobbins and gloves.

Perhaps there is a reflection of this in the current vogue for burying foundation deposits reflecting the current era, such as coins and newspapers, in public buildings, and the popularity of Millennium time capsules put together for people to find in the future.

Personal superstitions

Great care was taken over nails and hair, as people believed that if a witch obtained them she could incorporate them into images to wreak magic against her victim. In North Leigh hair was cut when the moon was waxing, so that it would grow quickly, and corns when the moon waned so that they shrank. At Bloxham cut hair was carefully collected: the Revd W. Fothergill Robinson had his hair cut in the garden one day in 1920, and told his servants not to put a cloth down, but they insisted, so that they could collect all the stray hair, for they thought that if any was picked up by birds he would have a headache.

It was lucky to cut nails before noon on a Monday, but bad luck after noon. At Kelmscott if you cut your nails on a Friday or Sunday the Devil would be with you all week. Significance was attached to white specks on nails: on the thumb it indicated a gift, on the first finger a friend, on the second finger a foe, on the third finger a sweetheart and on the fourth finger a journey to go.

Spitting reinforced binding oaths among boys at Finstock, who would 'spit their faith' on a stone, or spit on their hands before fighting to give shrewder blows, according to John Kibble.

Mollie Harris maintained that if you sneezed in Ducklington it indicated that you would be kissed, cursed, cussed or shake hands with a fool, so her mother would immediately shake hands with the sneezer to save him or her from being cursed. She also interpreted itching: if your nose itched you would:

> Run a mile
> Jump a stile, or
> Eat a pancake in a field.

If your ears itched or burned, someone was talking about you:

> Right your mother
> Left your lover.

If your hands itched:

> Scratch them on wood
> Sure to come good.

The Kidlington version ran:

> Scratch them on brick
> Sure to come quick.

Itching of the right hand indicated receipt of money, the left expenses; on the soles of the feet it indicated a walk on strange ground.

At North Leigh if two people dried their hands on the same towel they were bound to quarrel, and if two washed in the same water they must both make crosses over it. It was unlucky to give a friend a pair of gloves as you would shake hands and part. Eynsham people would put a coin in a pair of gloves when giving them as a present, and at North Leigh the same applied to giving a purse. If you left gloves at a friend's house, you must go back, sit down and put them on while standing before leaving, or you would never return to that house. At Launton it was bad luck to turn back but that was averted by sitting down, counting to ten and picking up your purse before starting out again.

At North Leigh it was bad luck to place new boots or shoes on the table. At Ducklington if new boots squeaked when first worn it indicated that they had not been paid for. A coin should be put in the pocket of a new suit or coat to avert bad luck.

Pins were vital for holding clothes together, and, until the nineteenth century, expensive because of the many processes involved in their manufacture, and intimately close to the wearer, which is perhaps why there are so many superstitions about them. At Spelsbury you should never pick up a pin with its point towards you. In Oxford:

> See a pin and let it lie,
> You'll want a pin before you die.

The Witney version ran:

> See a pin and pick it up,
> All the day you'll have good luck.

If your hairpins dropped out someone was thinking about you in Witney.

Household Superstitions

In Lower Heyford it was said that: 'You must get up early on 1 March and sweep the lintel of your door, and all round the hinges and frames and crevices, then, you'll be free from fleas coming into the house for whole year.' This was common practice until about 1890.

The hearth was the focus of the home, and black specks on the grate meant that a stranger was coming. In Charlbury women would not toss over a bed on Friday because it was unlucky or on Sunday because that was the Sabbath. Washing was taboo on Ash Wednesday or Good Friday, or someone would be washed out of the family as was washing blankets in May. Kelmscott people said:

> If you wash your blankets in May,
> You wash your family away.

While the Ducklington version ran:

> Wash blankets in May,
> You'll soon be under clay.

The dangers of going under a ladder were averted in Eynsham by crossing your fingers and keeping them crossed until you saw a donkey. It was lucky to encounter a sailor in uniform (particularly if one could touch his collar), a piebald horse or a loaded hay cart, upon which one should spit and make a wish. It was unlucky if one did not see these objects until they had already passed, and the hay cart should not be followed by a straw cart. To avert danger from meeting a cross-eyed person or exchanging glances with him, it was advisable to cross your fingers. Two people meeting on the stairs should touch each other to avert misfortune. At Kirtlington a hare's foot was often kept behind a stable door inside a horseshoe to bring good luck.

Belief in superstition has become attached to modern technology. A North Leigh man carried a stick on his tractor to beat it when it would not start, and another bit his recalcitrant tractor. In North Leigh it was said that a Rolls Royce car may fail to proceed, but will never break down, and you can stand a three-penny piece on the bonnet and the movement is so smooth that the coin will stay there when the car moves.

Food and Drink

At North Leigh one should never accept a penknife or anything that would cut as a gift without giving a penny in return, lest the friendship be broken. Crossed knives on a table are the sign of a quarrel, and at Eynsham, they said: 'Stir with a knife, stir up strife'. At Upper Heyford: if you drop a knife you will have a gentle-man visitor, if a fork, a lady and if a spoon a child. At Stoke Row to drop a spoon was to suffer disappointment, the larger the spoon the greater the loss. Seating thirteen at table was considered extremely unlucky.

A Good Friday loaf baked in 1897, now in the collection of the Oxfordshire Museums Service. Bread and hot-cross buns baked on Good Friday partook of the holiness of the day and were said never to go mouldy, and if kept in the house brought good luck and good health to those who inhabited it. Once the next year's loaf had been baked the old one was relegated to the medicine cabinet and used to cure stomach ailments.

Salt is incorruptible and preserves from decay so signifies eternity. At Eynsham it was said: 'Help you to salt, help you to sorrow', and that you can always catch birds if you put salt on their heads.

Baking was an important household task, and:

> If the woman had the head
> You'll never lack bread.

At North Leigh when the dough was placed in front of the fire to rise a cross was carved into it to stop the Devil from sitting on it. In Islip it was said that:

New bread, new beer and green wood will bring ruin to any man's house.

The first rhubarb should be eaten on Easter Sunday, while at Freeland apples were not eaten before St Swithun's day as they 'had not been baptised' and blackberries should not be eaten after 11 October as the Devil would have brushed his tail over them. At North Leigh hot elder wine was drunk on Christmas Day, the first figs on Palm Sunday and the first gooseberry on Whit Sunday. Pork was eaten on St Giles' Fair Sunday.

The Charlbury Flitch (a side of bacon) was presented to the man 'who minded his own business and no-one else's' for ten or twenty years. A man by the name of Huckins won it around 1825.

seven

SPORTS AND GAMES

Many entertainments have died out as customs and beliefs have changed, and many would be considered too rough or politically incorrect today. Sometimes they were an informal way of training labouring men for war, such as archery and quintain (the Tudors wanted their subjects to practise archery in preference to football, as they needed trained soldiers). Puritans disapproved of sports, but in 1618 and 1633 royal declarations advocated participation in them after Divine Service, encouraging archery, leaping, vaulting and dancing. Dr Plot, writing in 1676, described the quintain:

> They first set a post perpendicularly in the ground, and then place a slender piece of timber on the top of it, on a spindle, with a board nailed to one end, and a bag of sand hanging at the other – against this board they anciently rode with spears; now, as I saw it at Deddington … only with strong staves, which violently bring about the bag of sand, if they make not good speed away, it strikes them about the back or shoulders, and sometimes perhaps knocks them from their horses; the great design of the sport being to try the agility of both horse and man, and to break the board … this is now only in request at marriages, and set up in the way for young men to ride at as they carry home the bride, he that breaks the board being counted the best man.

Bull Baiting and Cock Fighting

Bull baiting was popular in Headington. In 1727 Oxford undergraduates rioted when local people objected to them tying a cat to a bull's tail. When the students were worsted, about five hundred reinforcements armed with clubs broke nearly all the windows in Headington, beating up people and stealing items. The last bull baiting in Charlbury was a fiasco: the bull escaped, and when captured would not fight the dogs so it was slaughtered. Bull baiting was still popular in Wheatley (where the bull, wearing a garland, was paraded down to West Field Road) in 1837, and at Wantage until 1835 when it was prohibited by law. Crowds came to watch the proceedings, together with pedlars, hawkers and gypsies. Bull baiting died out in Bicester around 1800 but badger baiting continued into the early nineteenth century in Charlbury and was popular with grooms and servants.

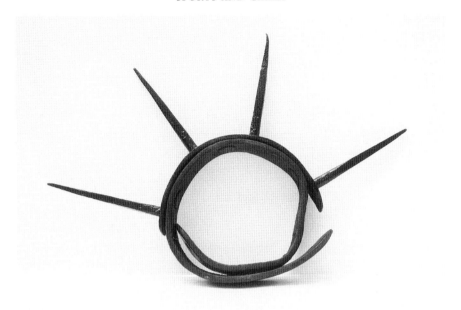

Leather dog collar with metal spikes, believed to have been used during bull-baiting in Bicester in the early nineteenth century. Historian John Dunkin recorded in *History of Bicester* (1816) that local magistrate and landowner John Coker had tried to put an end to the barbarous sport.

Cockpits were usually situated near inns: one operated in the attics of a large house in Market Square, Bicester until the mid-nineteenth century, and Woodstock still has a road called Cockpit Close.

Cutshins and kickshins

Cutshins and kickshins were violent contact sports popular in the Vale of White Horse. Cutshins was played by carters who stood a little apart and slashed at each other's legs with their whips until one gave in by shouting 'Hold!' The loser paid for the beer served at the midday meal.

Kickshins was potentially more dangerous as each man held on to his opponent's smock collar and kicked with hob-nailed boots at his shins, again the loser paying for the beer. The sport could lead to the men's shins becoming bent and twisted. At Filkins disputes were settled by shin kicking until the early nineteenth century. The participants soaked their boots in rainwater and let them dry in the sun to harden them.

Backswording and Wrestling

Backswording was more universally popular. In 1636 the Laudian Statutes prohibited members of the university from 'cudgel-playing', but this did not stop others partaking. In 1684 a reference in a pamphlet (MS *Top* Oxon d.201) described 'the

'The coolness and resolution in the faces of the two men, as they struck and parried with those heavy sticks, trying all the points of each others' play in a dozen rapid exchanges; the skill and power which every turn of the wrist showed, and the absolute indifference with which they treated any chance blow which fell on arm or shoulder made it a really grand sight.' Backswording depicted by Thomas Hughes in *Scouring of the White Horse*.

great Cudgel-playing at Cowley Wake, which is the Olympiad of that Country where John Pasmore of Hedington was the Hat and Feather'. In 1723 back-swording was performed at Wantage Fair:

> there was a very great match of backsword and cudgel playing between the hill-country and the vale-country. Berkshire men being famous for this sport or exercise. And 'tis remarkable that at Childrey, by Wantage, lives one old Vicars, a farmer, who hath been very excellent at it, and hath now five sons, that are so expert in it that 'tis supposed they are a match for any five in England. They always come off victors, and carry off the hat, the reward of the conqueror, so that they have not bought any hats since they have been celebrated for this exercise. (Reliquae Hearnianae, ii, 168)

Jackson's Oxford Journal advertised backswording at Bampton on 15 May 1753:

> This is to give notice that there will be five guineas play'd for at back-sword, on Wednesday in the Whitsun week at Bampton in Oxfordshire, by nine or eleven men on a side: but if the sides cannot be made, then that side that shews out shall have one guinea and the remainder to be play'd out at five shillings each head, and one shilling to the man that has his head broke.

Men played facing their opponents, armed with a cudgel, with their left hands strapped behind their backs, aiming to hit the top of the head, not the face, and the blood had to run down for an inch before a hit was counted.

In Hanborough in the early nineteenth-century backswording, singlestick and wrestling matches were organised by Jericho Hall, who dressed flamboyantly in knee breeches, blue stockings and buckle shoes and lived at the the Wrestling House, later changed to the 'Rosslin House'.

According to Thomas Hughes in *Scouring of the White Horse*, by the mid-nineteenth century contact sports were going out of fashion:

> We wish to say a few words, my men, to those who are going to play with the sticks or wrestle today. There has been a good deal of talk about these sports … and many persons think they shouldn't be allowed at all now-a-days – that the time for them has gone by. They say, that men always lose their tempers and get brutal at these sports. We have settled however to give the old-fashioned games a fair trial; and it will rest with yourselves whether we shall ever be able to offer prizes for them again. For depend upon it, if there is any savage work to-day, if you lose your tempers, and strike or kick one another unfairly, you will never see any more wrestling or backsword on White Horse Hill.

Jingling

Jingling was popular in Moreton in the Vale of White Horse until 1860. Two blindfolded men were placed inside a pen made from hurdles, one carrying a bell and the other trying to find him from the sound he made. The sport was also popular at the Scouring of the White Horse, but Thomas Hughes was not impressed:

> I thought this the slowest game I saw. The ring must have been forty yards across, or thereabouts, and there were only eight blindfolded men running after the bellman. To make it good fun there should have been twenty-five or thirty at least. Then the bellman, who has his hands tied behind him, ought to have the bell tied round his neck, or somewhere where he can't get at it to stop the ringing; but our bellman had the bell tied to his waistband behind, so that he could catch hold of it when he was in danger. Then half the men could see, I'm sure, by the way they carried their heads up in the air, especially one gipsy, who, I think, won the prize at last. The men who couldn't see were worth watching, for they kept catching and tumbling over one other.

Pub Games

The quintessentially Oxfordshire pub game is Aunt Sally, which may have replaced shying at cocks, and is said by some players to date back to the fifteenth century. Fairgrounds had Aunt Sally games where the target was a clay pipe in the mouth of a black female doll's face but the current 'Sally' is a round piece of wood with a face marked on, placed on a metal stand. Eight players form each team, and each player has six sticks approximately the size of a rolling pin to throw, aiming to knock the head off, without touching the stand, each time, giving a maximum score for each leg of forty-eight, and a match consists of three legs. An umpire oversees proceedings and someone else replaces the fallen head. An Aunt Sally league still exists in Oxfordshire and Aunt Sally was one of the pub games included in the inaugural English Pub Games Championship in 2004 at Ditchley Park, which included marbles, skittles, ring tennis, three-legged races, shove halfpenny, dominoes, short mat bowls, horse shoe throwing, tiddlywinks, darts and crib.

George Swinford recalled three quoits beds in Filkins. Two holes were dug one foot deep and two yards square, twenty yards apart, which were filled with clay and an iron peg was stuck in the centre. Each player had two steel quoits, diameter about six inches, weighing about two pounds, which were dropped over the peg, or as close to it as possible. A quoit which dropped over the peg was a 'ringer' which gained two points, the next closest got one point. The game died out around 1900 in Filkins, but carried on until the late twentieth century in some places such as Stoke Row. At Berrick Salome the quoits were flat on one side and curved the other, and if the quoit fell on the curved side it was known as 'the lady'.

Another Filkins game was bandy, which resembled hockey. Sticks were gathered from the hedgerows and the ball used, the nunney, was a block of elm the size of a hen's egg, which was hit from wall to wall or hedge to hedge. If a player covered the nunney with his foot his opponents shouted 'Turn, Bumby!', and he was liable to be hit if he did not get out of the way. Bandy was replaced by football in Filkins in 1898.

Children's Games

Poor country children had to be inventive in finding toys: marbles could be obtained by breaking spruce bottles and taking out the glass ball in the neck, and children living near Witney could persuade elder siblings to get string for their tops or skipping ropes from the blanket factories. Fivestones was played at Lower Heyford with rhyconella fossils or little stones called dabs. Conkers were readily accessible in autumn; an Oxford conker rhyme was quoted by Iona and Peter Opie in *Children's Games in Street and Playground*:

> Iddy, iddy, onker,
> My first conker,
> Iddy, iddy oh,
> My first go.

Kingham children sometimes used small shells known as guggles in place of conkers.

There was a seasonal flavour to games: at Great Tew hoops and skipping started when the roads cleared after the winter, and drier weather encouraged hopscotch in Ducklington, where two forms were played, one on a bed of six large squares, each with a number chalked inside. A small flattish stone was kicked from one square to the next while hopping on one foot. If the stone slid too far or landed on a line, the player had to start again. A more difficult version was played on a large spiral bed, with complex instructions written in each segment.

Girls and boys played with glass and clay marbles, glass ones considered far more valuable (two stone or clay equalled one glass at Bicester, while two glass equalled one coloured, known as an alley). Large marbles were called balchers at Lower Heyford. At Great Tew a ring was made with a hole in the centre and the aim was to knock as many marbles out of the hole as possible.

There were many types of tops including peg tops, which were flung using coiled string, and spinning Jennies, while Sid Hedges mentioned squats, diggles, plump Germans, slim and French window-breakers in *Bicester wuz a Little Town*.

Skipping was universally popular with the girls; rhymes accompanying skipping at Lower Heyford included:

> Salt, mustard, vinegar, pepper

And:

> Handy, pandy, sugar candy, French helm and rock

A Lower Heyford ball game involved throwing a ball three times against a wall and catching it, throwing it three times again touching your head while the ball

Mrs Thomas Scrivener outside her Fancy Goods and Toy Shop in Bicester in about 1910, with hoops in various sizes for children of different ages displayed outside. Boys played with blacksmith-made iron hoops which had a hook to bowl them along, while girls had wooden hoops with sticks.

was in the air, then three times touching the shoulders, then touching knees and turning round. In Bat-a-ball-base, a sort of rounders, one team stood in a row while the other team fielded. The bowler threw the ball at one of the team who had to hit it with her hand. If the fielder could pick it up and hit the girl she was out. When all the team were out they changed roles. Ducklington children played Alary: chanting:

> One, two, three, Alary,
> My ball went down the cary.
> Serves you right for playing alary,
> On a Sunday morning.

The ball was bounced the first time each word of the rhyme was spoken, but the second time the right leg was thrown over the bouncing ball, then it was bounced with the left hand and the left leg thrown over it. Girls spent ages perfecting their skills.

Tip cat was a piece of wood about four inches long, pointed at each end, which was tapped, spun up and hit with a stick while a second person ran down to a den before the stick hit the ground at Great Tew, while at Bicester the aim was to hit the stick as far as possible.

John Aubrey recorded leap-candle in Oxford: girls put a candle in a candlestick in the middle of the room and lifted up their clothes to dance backwards and forwards over it singing:

> The tailor of Bicister,
> He has but one eye,
> He cannot cut a pair of green galagaskins,
> If he were to try.

Flora Thompson described in *Lark Rise to Candleford* how girls seemed to change personality while playing ring games:

> Most of the girls when playing revealed graces unsuspected in them at other times; their movements became dignified and their voices softer and sweeter than ordinarily, and when hauteur was demanded by the part, they became, as they would have said, 'regular duchesses'. It was probable that carriage and voice inflexion had been handed down with the words.

Flora thought that the ring games were dying out in the late nineteenth century, but they survived for another hundred years or so, although they are rare in the twenty-first century. Many types have been recorded, and the same games were played in many places, often with slight variations. A ring game from Headington recorded in G.A. Coppock's *Headington Quarry and Shotover* ran:

> On the mountain stands a lady,
> Who she is I do not know.
> All she wants is gold and silver.
> All she wants is a nice young man.

'Madam will you walk. Madam will you talk.
Madam will you walk and talk with me?'
[The girl in the centre answers] 'No.'
'Not if I buy you an easy chair
To sit in the garden and take fresh air?
Madam will you walk …'
[Response] 'No'
'Not if I buy you a nice straw hat
With six yards of ribbon hanging from the back?'
'No.'
'Not if I bring you a nice bunch of keys
To let you in wherever you please?'
'Yes!'

In 'Queen Anne' from Lower Heyford, described by Dorothy Dew, the first team, which had the ball, said: 'Queen Ann, Queen Anne she sits in the sun as fair as a lily as bright as one.' Second team: 'Turn maids all.' First team: 'The more we turn, the more we may. Queen Anne was born on Michaelmas Day, we've brought you three letters for you to read one.' The second team had to guess which girl held the ball. Second team: 'We can't read the one unless we read all, so please so-and-so, give us the ball.' The girl with the ball revealed it, and the first team responded: 'The ball is yours' if the second team had guessed right or 'ours' if they had guessed wrong, continuing: 'so we will go and gather some gilly flowers.' If the second team had guessed wrong the girls went through the whole procedure again, if they had guessed right, the teams swapped roles.

In 'Queen Caroline' a game played by Mollie Harris in Ducklington six or seven girls linked arms across the road and sang:

Queen, Queen Caroline,
Dipped her hair in the turpentine,
The turpentine made it shine,
Queen, Queen, Caroline.

A popular boys' game in Ducklington described by Mollie Harris was Fox and Hounds. On frosty winter nights they ran for miles, chasing a boy chosen as the fox. The 'hounds' shouted 'Come out, wherever you are, the dogs are on your trail.' The fox would sometimes 'holler' to indicate his whereabouts, and sometimes double back to confuse his pursuers. If he was not caught the first night, the game might continue until he was caught, when another boy would take his place.

Unfortunately, with the growing poplularity of computer games, many traditional games have died out.

eight

THE NATURAL WORLD

Holy Wells

Water has always been vital for life, and wells were important sources of water. Neolithic people are thought to have regarded some wells as sacred, as ritual pits associated with water worship have been found near them. During the Iron Age wells were sometimes associated with the head cult, connected with fertility, prophecy and healing. Pagan wells sometimes became Christian holy wells, often dedicated to saints.

St Margaret's Well at Binsey, near Oxford, traditionally sprang up when St Frideswide prayed for water when fleeing Oxford. During the middle ages it was a renowned healing well and may have been decked with flowers. It was famous for curing the lame, and had oracular powers to ease emotional burdens. Queen Katherine of Aragon visited it in pilgrimage to pray for a son. Although well-worship was banned at the Reformation, it did not disappear: in 1893 pins

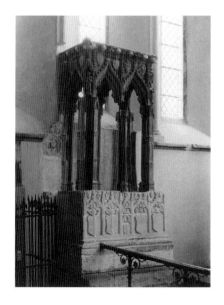

The shrine of St Edburg, an Anglo-Saxon princess, probably the daughter of King Penda of Mercia, who was a nun in Adderbury in the seventh century. In the early fourteenth century her bones were installed in a shrine in Bicester Priory which was moved to Stanton Harcourt church, where parts of it stand on a limestone base in the chancel. A sacred well dedicated to her in Bicester, used for curing sore eyes, was approached down a processional way known as St Edburga's Walk.

were discovered on a ledge at the well, perhaps to request help, or in thanks. St Margaret's well is the origin of Lewis Carroll's Treacle Well, as treacle is derived from 'trickle', the medieval word for beneficial or healing.

St Bartholomew's Well near the Cowley Road was popular among under-graduates, and had the nearest ceremonial found in Oxfordshire to Derbyshire well-dressing. Anthony Wood described New College students processing there on May Day in the early seventeenth century to welcome spring 'with their lords and ladyes, garlands, fifs, flutes and drums to salute the great goddess Flora and to attribute her all prais with dancing and music'. Later this event was transferred to Ascension Day to prevent fights between New College and Magdalen College students. Anthony Wood said that the church was decorated with seasonal fruits and that during the service: '… the fellows went one by one up to the altar where stood a certaine vessel deckt with Inttyes [nosegays], and therin offered a piece of silver which is afterwards divided among the poore men [almsmen of St Bartholomew's leper hospital].' They walked up the path to Strowell (which was strewn with flowers), and after the epistle and gospel had been read, sang May songs. The Chapel was visited again at Whitsun for 'Bringing in the Fly', when college cooks processed to the decorated well, captured a cranefly and brought it back in a cage amidst much drinking and hilarity to the colleges, which had their gateways decorated with green boughs.

Aristotle's Well, east of the Oxford Canal near Heyfields Bridge, was also known as Brummans Well. People drank the water and made a secret wish, leaving a penny for the guardian of the well. Water from the well was mixed with sugar for drinks until about 1880, and in 1718 the winners of student games played on Ash Wednesday left trophies at the well.

St Edmund's or St Edward's Well in St Clements parish was so popular that in 1290 and 1304 the archdeacon commanded that it should not be venerated. However in the seventeenth century Dr Plot wrote that although it had been destroyed, older people remembered that it was 'believed to be effectual in curing divers Distempers, and thereupon held to be of so great Sanctity, that here they made Vow, and brought with them Alms and Offerings.' Dr Rawlinson, principle of St Edmund Hall, erected a house near the Crowell Well in Oxford, decorated with the motto:

> No man will hurt this well that's wise,
> For this hurts none, but cures the eyes.
> None but will hurt this well that's wise,
> For it helps none, but hurts the wise.

Wychwood Forest was famous for the Iron Well near Leafield. People processed there on Palm Sunday or Easter Monday, armed with bottles containing liquorice sticks to fill them with water from the Iron or Uzzel Well to make Spanish water. In the 1950s children used to take twelve ounce bottles containing small pieces of liquorice, brown sugar and peppermint or lemon sweets to fill. At Spelsbury water from the holy well was used for baptisms. Otmoor boasted several wells. Blackwater wells at Charlton-on-Otmoor, and Oddington were used to treat sore eyes and eczema and protect cattle against 'moor evil' and the well at Noke helped sore eyes.

Legends grew up that the Virgin Mary visited a well at Bampton to perform her ablutions, so it became a place of pilgrimage as people came to be dipped in well water to cure many ailments. Many wells such as, Granny Well at Wardington, Appleford well, Sunningwell, Princess Elizabeth's well at Bisham, Colwell Spring at Dorchester, Old Moll on Shotover, Jenny Newton's well near Holywell in Oxford, Holy Well at Rycote and Black Jack spring at Kingston Lisle were used to treat sore eyes. Chilswell was said to aid fertility, at Goring a spring helped skin diseases, and St Anthony's well at Wittenham was used by the sick and dying.

Weather Lore

Country people were thought to be attuned to local conditions which foretold the weather. Some local adages were written down in 1744 by the 'Shepherd of Banbury', including:

> A red evening and grey morning sets the Pilgrim a walking

And:

> If woolly fleeces spread the Heavenly Way,
> Be sure no rain disturbs the Summer Day.

And:

> When Clouds appear like Rocks and Towers,
> The Earth's refresh'd by frequent Showers.

The famous rhyme:

> Red sky at night, shepherd's delight,
> Red sky in the morning, shepherd's warning

was used at Great Tew, while at Minster Lovell a red sky in the morning which persisted or veered south meant rain, if it moved west the weather would be fine and windy.

Birds' behaviour at Minster Lovell could indicate rain, for example if blackbirds tweedled, birds sang on a dull November morning, or the green woodpecker was noisy. At Spelsbury when rooks dropped and flew wildly weather would be bad. Robins whistling in August at Berrick Salome indicated a hard winter. Swallows flying high at Beckley promised good weather. Other indicators were thrushes keeping near the hedges, wagtails near farm buildings and peacocks screeching.

Animal behaviour also provided clues: if mouseholes in the hedgerows at Great Tew faced north, the winter would be mild; if the cows and sheep lay down (at Beckley) fine weather was expected or cattle stood on high ground (at Kencott) weather would be fine. At Minster Lovell they said that when the cat sat with its back to the fire or caterpillars crawled up posts there would be frost. Snails creeping up tree trunks and telegraph poles foretold warm weather. Snow was forecast by birds seeking shelter in the woods. If snow lay on the ground for three days more was on the way. Sharp frosts before Christmas meant rain afterwards, but

> If the ice before Christmas will bear a duck,
> There is nothing after but slush and muck.

Calendar dates were indicators. At Forest Hill 2 February was a significant date:

> If Candlemas Day be dry and fair,
> The half o' winter's to come and mair;
> If Candlemas Day be wet and foul,
> The half o' winter's gone at Yule.

The weather on the solstice on 21 March foretold conditions for the next three months, while 'a rainy Easter betokens a good harvest', but in Stratton Audley it meant a wet summer:

> Rain Easter Day,
> Plenty of grass but little good hay.

In Wheatley St Swithun's Day, 1 July, was called 'Apple Christening Day', and if it rained that day the apples were christened and would develop well, otherwise they would not flourish.

In North Oxfordshire the wind direction at midnight on the eve of Deddington Fair (22 November) would continue for the rest of the year. If the sun shone on Christmas Day it indicated a good harvest. A 'green Christmas means a full churchyard', suggested that warm weather at the end of the year would be followed by bitter cold. Rain or snow was important in February:

> February fill-dyke, either black or white, but if it be white, it's the best to like.

Mist foretold future conditions, as Elsie Corbett wrote in *A History of Spelsbury*:

> When the mist rises o'er the hill
> There will be water for the mill;
> When the mist rises from the hollow
> There will be a fine day tomorrow.
> The hours between twelve and two
> Will show what the day will do.
> When the cock crows on going to bed
> He'll wake in the morning with a watery head.

At Chipping Norton it was said:

> Mist in the 'ollow
> Fine on the morrow.

Winter thunderstorms foretold a bad summer, and:

> A storm out of season is a summer's glory or a great man's death.

Thunder was feared: during a thunderstorm all knives should be put away, mirrors were covered and radios switched off. Fossil belemnites were believed to be thunderbolts fallen from the sky during storms, in reality heavy rain washed them out of the Oxford Clay. Rainbows had ambivalent meanings:

> A Rainbow in the morning is the Shepherd's warning.
> A Rainbow at night is the Shepherd's delight.

While it was considered unlucky to point at a rainbow, one should make a wish on seeing one.

The moon is thought to exert great influence over weather, which changes with the new moon. At Filkins:

> If the new moon lies on her back, it will be fine. She is
>   holding back the rain.

A contrary view was held in Oxford:

> If the new moon lies on her back, it will be wet.

A halo round the moon indicated bad weather, and the further the halo was from the moon, the sooner the rain would come. Two new moons in May indicated appalling weather:

> Two moons in May, it will rain for a year and a day.

The new moon was the time of hardest frosts.

The aurora borealis is seldom seen as far south as Oxfordshire, but when it is, it is ill-omened, presaging war, as it was seen before the Boer War and the First World War.

The advent of a new century was thought to bring change in the weather: bad summers at the middle of the twentieth century were attributed to the Earth turning towards the sun for the first half of the century and away during the second half.

Animals, Birds and Insects

At North Leigh it was lucky if a newborn calf sneezed, but white cows, particularly shorthorns, were considered no good. The copper rings fastened through cows' dewlaps were thought to ward off disease.

At Bicester it was thought that if a horse had a white foot, the white might go through the hoof and make it softer and more liable to infection, hence the rhyme:

> One white foot buy him,
> Two white feet try him,
> Three white feet look well about him,
> Four white feet go home without him.

A dog howling persistently was a death omen, but a spayed bitch could avert evil spirits. At Steeple Barton a cure for whooping cough was to cut some hair from the patient's neck and give it to a dog to eat. If a cat coughed at Yarnton, everyone in the house would cough in turn, so the cat must be put outside immediately. At Berrick Salome kittens born at harvest were better at catching rats and mice, while May kittens were hopeless.

Rabbits were well-thought of in Oxfordshire, hence the local curse: 'May all your rabbits be dead.' A hare's foot was sometimes, as at Kirtlington, kept inside a stable door with a horseshoe to bring good luck. At Didcot they said that if you had a toad in the garden you would never be short of water.

There are a number of local names for birds:

Acho	green woodpecker
Bum barrel	lapwing
Dishwasher	wagtail
Hedge-Betty	hedge sparrow
Hern or heron crow	heron
Horsematch:	wheatear (because it flew alongside carriages as though racing them)
Mollern or Mollyarn	heron
Musky	sparrow
Peafinch	chaffinch
Quick-me-dick or twit-me-dick	quail
Rainbird	green woodpecker
Sea crow	seagull
Spadjuck or spadgick	sparrow
Tom	cockerel
Thresher	thrush

The crowing of the cockerel at midnight was considered a death omen; if it crowed during the night, an angel was passing; if it crowed near the door, a visitor was coming.

In Headington two crows flying over a house indicated that there would soon be a birth. To see one crow was bad luck and foretold calamity. Mollie Harris said that in Ducklington people recited the following rhyme on seeing crows:

One for sorrow,
Two for joy,
Three for a girl,
Four for a boy,
Five for silver,
Six for gold,
Seven for a secret never to be told.

Such rhymes are more usually applied to magpies. Mollie Harris said that it was bad luck to meet one if one did not say 'Good morning, sir' and nod one's head.

In other places one should bow to the magpie or spit. In Banbury the rhyme given above for crows was applied to magpies and an alternative was:

> One sorrow,
> Two joy,
> Three a wedding,
> Four a boy,
> Five a sickening,
> Seven a dance,
> Eight a lady goes to France.

In Watlington the magpie was only considered unlucky if it was flying to the left.

The arrival of the cuckoo heralded the summer, and some country people believed that instead of migrating in the winter they turned into sparrowhawks for the cold season. In Banbury it was lucky to have money in your pocket when you saw the first cuckoo of the year, but if your pockets were empty it indicated poverty. It was lucky to see a kingfisher while travelling.

Rooks building their nests high up presaged a good summer but if they suddenly deserted an elm tree it was diseased and would shortly fall. Martins were widely considered to bring money. Swallows nesting on a house was considered very lucky, and the nest must not be damaged. It was said that swallows fly high before fine weather and low before rain.

Swan Upping at Benson and Shillingford in July 2002. Around 600 cygnets are examined each year; those of mixed parentage are marked half for the cob, half the pen, and odd cygnets are allocated to the cob.

Swans are owned by the monarch, the Seigneur of Swans, and all unmarked swans on open water belong to the Crown (they have remained unmarked since this was requested by Queen Alexandra). The City Livery Companies of the Vintners and Dyers were each granted the privilege of owning a 'game' of swans around 1493, and their cygnets are marked annually to distinguish them from those belonging to the Crown. Swan Upping is done on the River Thames between Southwark Bridge and Henley-on-Thames over six days in July by three Swan Herdsmen: the Queen's Swankeeper and one each from the Vintners and Dyers, who wear gold-braided uniforms. The cygnets of the Dyers are marked with one nick on the beak and the Vintners with two.

Plant lore

Oxfordshire wild flowers names include:

Adam's cloth	red campion
Angel's eyes	speedwell
Blue butcher or bloody butcher	blue orchis
Boys and girls	lungwort
Champs	field mushrooms
Coddle-apple	great hairy willowherb
Fuzz	furze
Half-wood	woody nightshade
Keck or lady's lace	cow parsley
Keys of heaven	cowslip
Kiss behind the garden gate	London pride
Kiss-me-quick	tansy
Marshmallow	kingcup
Mayblobs	kingcups
Neighbour	valerian
Old man	southernwood
Old woman	wormwood
Pillidillies	daisies
Queen Anne's lace	cow parsley
Scabby-heads	cow parsley
Slans	sloes
Soldiers and sailors	lungwort
Turn again gentleman	Turk's head lily
Water buttercup	kingcup
Water bubbles	marsh marigolds

Flowers blooming out of season were considered unlucky. It was felt that picking dead flowers by the roadside could lead to sickness. Neither cuckoo flowers nor poppies should be brought indoors, and in Heyford they said you would go blind if you looked into the heart of a poppy. Snowdrops should never be brought into the house, as they 'wear a shroud' and are a sure sign of an imminent funeral. John Aubrey wrote that young men who had lost their sweethearts to another man wore willow garlands as a sign of grief.

The elder is widely connected with witchcraft, and in Beckley it was thought that if you burned elder wood you would become bewitched and elder should never be cut down. At Wootton it was never made into a wattle hedge as that could give power to witches but it kept flies away if tied to horses' heads. Lilac was unlucky and was never given to the sick.

Parsley should be planted by a woman, as a man had to go to hell to ask permission for it to grow, so took a long time to germinate. If given parsley, it should always be planted by the donor. It should never be transplanted, as that would cause the death of the person who transplanted it, or someone connected with him. It should preferably be planted on Good Friday, when it came under the protection of God.

The Pasque flower or purple anemone is said to grow where Saxon blood has been shed. The Persicaria flower has a dark spot in the centre of each leaf, traditionally acquired when it grew below the cross on which Christ was cruci-fied, and drops of His blood fell on it. In Oxfordshire it was said that the Virgin Mary used its leaves to make an ointment, but on one occasion she could not find it, and was so cross that she named it an ordinary weed, as explained in the rhyme:

> She could not find in time of need,
> And so she pinched it for a weed.

In this story the marks are where she pinched it with her fingers.

Sage, rosemary and lavender are all 'feminine' plants which thrive when the woman rules the house. A Charlbury man cut down a vigorous sage bush lest people thought he was ruled by his wife. In North Leigh it is said that when sage is in bloom the wife is master. Others say sage will not flourish unless it grows from a stolen cutting. Clary or wild sage is said to have been dropped by Roman soldiers, as it is often found near Roman roads. Rosemary's meaning is remem-brance and it was often dropped into graves at funerals.

Wormwood (old man) should never be planted next to Southernwood (old woman) as the old woman will kill the old man. Young people in Cowley whispered into yew trees when they were in berry and hoped to hear responses from their lovers.

Folk Medicine

Until the advent of the National Health Service many people could ill afford doc-tors' fees so many home-made remedies were used to treat patients, some of which were passed down over generations. Some women who had special herbal skills such as Elizabeth Cracklow of Adderbury set up as wisewomen. She was consulted in 1546 by a man whose arm was out of joint and got her husband to preach over the arm, then made the sign of a cross over it and got her husband to say 'God's for-bade'. Some remedies were religious in origin such as the belief that a touch from the sacred hand of the king could cure scrofula, the 'King's Evil'. In 1687 James II visited Banbury and Anne Watts of Cropredy, Richard Davis of Williamscot, James Meacock and Isabell — (surname missing) were granted certificates by their vicars to recommend that they should be touched by the king. Whether the cure was effective or not is not recorded. The cure for leprosy (in the *Gentleman's Magazine* of September 1866) from Clattercote, which had a leper hospital, may be very old:

Take powder of burnt hedgehog's flesh. Take marjoram, bayberries, the seeds of lice-bane, of each five ounces; the earth called sinopida, five ounces; then seethe them all together; then bathe there – with the space of five or six days, twice a day. In bathing is the body to be rubbed with black sope.

Votive offerings were used by the Romans and more recently a limestone head of a leper and a limestone plaque in the shape of a human ear have been used as offerings. Such items were often presented to saints in an effort to cure disease. Around 1900 an Oxford man carried a piece of flint resembling a swollen foot and leg around with him to prevent gout. Powder from fossil belemnites, mixed with water, was used in the nineteenth century to treat eruptions of the lips. Belemnites were considered to have celestial origins, but it may have been the calcareous matter in them which proved effective.

Whooping cough was rampant, and there were many suggested cures. One was to slice a turnip, cover the slices with brown sugar and leave overnight, then give the resulting juices to the patient. In Goring a desperate father heated milk and gave it to his ferret to drink, giving the milk left by the ferret to his child. An alternative was to catch nine mice, fry them and give three each night to the patient. An old shepherd recommended taking the child at four o'clock each morning to the sheepfold when the air was hot and steamy. At Charlbury an afflicted child was passed nine times over and under a piebald horse. At Aston Rowant if a child with whooping cough was sick, a dog was persuaded to eat the sick, and it was thought that the disease would be transferred to the dog. At Drayton a few white hairs from the chest of a donkey were placed on the patient. Another remedy was to take the child into the fields and find a branch bent back and rooted into the ground in an arch and pass the child nine times beneath it on nine mornings; a bramble from Horspath used in this way is housed in the Pitt Rivers Museum. The aim was to pass the disease to the earth, while the thorns prevented it from returning to the child. Chastleton women used to carry babies with whooping cough nine times round the church on three successive Fridays to cure them, but on one occasion two of the babies died after the first church circuiting and the practice was given up.

Cures for warts often involved rubbing the wart and attempting to transfer it to something else, such as rubbing it with the white inner lining of a broad bean pod and throwing the pod away or burying it in a secret place. As the pod rotted the wart would disappear. An alternative was to carry around a piece of bacon fat – as it dried the wart would disappear, or, as at Spelsbury, rub bacon fat on the wart, then bury it in an ant hill or rub it on a snail. Other Spelsbury cures were to rub the wart with a piece of stolen meat or with the third joint of a wheat straw. At Ducklington an old lady rubbed warts with a huge black slug. Some people stuck pins in a rowan tree (regarded as protective against witchcraft) and as the bark grew over them the warts should disappear. Slits could be cut in walnut or elder leaves and the leaves dropped down a well, and as they decayed the warts would go. A herbal cure was to rub the wart with the juice of milkweed, dandelion or yellow celandine.

C.M. Pumphrey wrote about a Charlbury child who had a wart pushing out her thumb nail. The doctor charmed it away by rubbing it, three times this way and three that, forming a cross, repeating words in a strange language, probably Latin, then tossed his hand over his left shoulder and told her not to worry about it any more because it would soon disappear, and it did. An old woman in Ferry Hinksey in the late nineteenth century asked patients how many warts they had, then produced a notched stick. She marked the sign of a cross on the largest wart then buried the stick in the garden and dismissed the patient, who reported that from that moment they began to crumble away. He was instructed not to tell anyone about the treatment or offer any remuneration until the warts had completely disappeared. John Mortimer, who worked as gardener at the Rectory at Lower Heyford in the mid-twentieth century was a wart charmer. Charmers keep their methods a closely guarded secret and pass them down from one generation to the next. Once the secret has been passed on, it can no longer be used by the person who passed it on.

Rheumatism could be cured by stealing a new potato, or taking a conker or nutmeg and keeping it in a pocket. It could be cured by chewing parsley or celery or thrashing the affected area with stinging nettles, or eating young dande-lion leaves mixed with vinegar. Some people wore little leather bags round their necks, with mysterious contents to protect against it.

Coughs and colds abound, as do cures for them. In Ducklington young patients were treated to a steaming basin of bread and milk, while older ones had home-made wine, often elderberry, heated with a red hot poker or black-currant tea made by putting a teaspoon of blackcurrant jam in a cup of boiling water. At Forest Hill a pint of boiled milk mixed with a tablespoon of flour and black treacle was consumed before going to bed. Raspberry vinegar was also effective, as was onion gruel used at Great Tew. A nose inflamed by a cold was rubbed with a tallow candle. For a bad cough a jar of gas tar was placed under the bed and a tar cord worn round the neck. In Ducklington it was thought that the fumes from a boiling hot tar barrel such as those used for road-building would break the phlegm of a cough. It was common for goose grease to be rubbed on children's chests to cure coughs, and many thought that any lotion used for coughs should also be applied to the soles of the feet as well as the chest. Sometimes tallow from a candle or goose grease was applied to brown paper and tied round the neck or chest. A Standlake woman recalled in 1955 that as a child she had a thick brown paper heart rubbed with grease from a tallow candle hung round her neck under her clothes, and as her cough improved little pieces of it were cut off until the cough had gone. Grease from church bells had additional holy power and was good for treating shingles and ringworm. A Ducklington girl with a weak chest had a narrow black velvet band fastened round her neck which she wore for many years and only took off when she washed.

John Kibble was told as a child that toothache was cured by worms in the teeth which could be extracted by putting henbane seeds in a basin and pouring boil-ing water over them, then inhaling (heat causes the henbane seeds to explode to resemble tiny maggots). A simpler Witney cure was to put a sock or stocking onto the left leg first. The roast parings of a turnip could be placed behind the ear, or, at Ducklington, a bag of heated salt held against the jaw eased toothache. Deafness could be treated by skinning a hedgehog and dipping the fat in cotton wool which was placed in the ears overnight. A hot roasted onion could be placed in the ear to ease pain.

Chilblains were beaten with a holly bush to let the chilled blood out, or rubbed with an ointment containing deadly nightshade juice mixed with lard, or at Ducklington rubbed with raw onions to ease itching.

Mollie Harris said that styes were treated in Ducklington by drawing a small piece of silk through a gold wedding ring, then stroking the stye with it twelve times night and morning. At North Leigh if a man wore a ring it was assumed that he wore it to ward off fits; in Oxford silver coins were specially made into rings by a jeweller and worn on a particular finger for this purpose.

Headache was treated by secretly taking a feather and wearing it on a hat or bonnet at Wootton, and at Forest Hill the answer was to capture and kill a snake, skin it and sew the skin inside your hat.

A Standlake child was bitten by a viper: the doctor instructed that the snake should be captured and killed and its fat rubbed on the boy, who survived. An eighteenth-century cure for the bite of a mad dog, purchased from Tarquin by George Cobb of Adderbury (recorded in the parish register of Balsham church in Cambridgeshire) consisted of twenty four grains of Cinnabar [a red crystalline form of mercuric sulphide] and fifteen grains of musk [stimulant and anti-spasmodic] pounded together and administered in rum, brandy or arrach, given as soon as possible after the bite and thirty days later, or if the symptoms have started, a second dose should be taken an hour after the first. Wasp stings were treated at Forest Hill by moistening a match head (not a safety match) with the mouth and rubbing well into the sting.

Cramp could be cured by stealing a piece of brimstone and secretly hiding it under the pillow. In Hook Norton five corks tied in a ring were placed at the foot of the bed to prevent cramp. Alternatively slippers were placed upside down under the bed.

John Kibble recorded that a woman with an enlarged neck had requested a few hairs from the tail of a stallion, (not revealing why she wanted them, as that would break the spell), which she wore tied round her neck to make the goitre disappear. In the late nineteenth century a girl from Forest Hill was taken to a hanging in Oxford to have a wen on her throat stroked nine times with the dead man's hand in one direction and nine times in another. She said several people wanted to have that done, but the man's relatives objected so it was not possible. Mumps or swollen glands were treated with marshmallow leaves soaked in boiling water.

A fresh warm cowpat was used in a poultice to cure gatherings and ease pain for cancer and tumours. To cure baldness a cowpat could be placed in a handkerchief and tied to the head overnight. An alternative was to rub the bare patch with a raw onion until the skin reddened then smear it with honey or wash the head frequently in a decoction of boxwood.

Sheeps' dung or bumbles were rolled into pills given to promote good health. Live sheep ticks were swallowed on nine successive mornings to cure ague and sheep's wool could be rubbed on corns to ease them. Ague was also treated by making a plaster of treacle and soot and applying it to each wrist, or swallowing six pills made from rolled cobweb. Eating roast mice was said to cure bedwetting (as did dandelion milk), while cobwebs were put on cuts to slow bleeding or rolled into pills given to cure insomnia. A child with worms was treated by a gipsy woman who said that she must take the largest worm that came out of her, bake it and drink it in milk, which cured her.

Spittle and massage was used to cure a child born with a crooked leg, and was rubbed onto ringworm with the forefinger of the right hand, which was otherwise considered unlucky to use as it was thought of as the 'poison finger'.

nine

SEASONAL CUSTOMS

When we are constantly bombarded by the media, it is hard to realise how important the role of seasonal customs was in providing a framework and structure for the year by which other tasks such as farming could be regulated, enabling people to entertain themselves, and providing a sense of community, where the poor were helped by the rich in the days before a welfare state. Beliefs and traditions changed according to the religious beliefs and morals of the time, but they gave a sense of continuity which we are in danger of losing today.

New Year

It was important to start the New Year in the right way as an augury for the rest of the year: a Bodicote man brought a sprig of greenery into the house as the church bells rang at midnight. Many people poured away any water in the house to replace it with freshly drawn water from the well. Some followed the Scottish custom of first footing, where the first person to enter the house after midnight should be a dark haired one bearing a piece of coal, bread, money and salt, to magically ensure that the family would go short of none of these in the coming year. Kencott people brought in coal first thing in the morning, leaving coal outside the front door for that purpose. In Burford the boys had a rhyme for New Year:

> I wish you a merry Christmas, a happy New Year,
> A pocket full of money and a cellar full of beer;
> A good fat pig to last you all the year,
> Please to give me New Year's Gift.

Twelfth Night

Twelfth Night marked the end of the Twelve Days of Christmas, at one time an agricultural holiday. Before the Victorians invented the 'family' Christmas, it was the time for riotous parties, dominated by an enormous cake in which were baked a bean and pea. The person who discovered the bean became king of the festivities and the finder of the pea the queen. Bakers advertised their magnificent Twelfth Night cakes. It was also the day to take down and burn Christmas evergreens.

Candlemas Day: 2 February

The Christian festival of Candlemas has been celebrated since the seventh century. Parishioners brought their candles to church to be blessed and sprinkled with holy water to frighten away devils, a rite banned at the Reformation. By Candlemas it should be light enough to eat the evening meal without lighting candles, as suggested in the Stratton Audley rhyme:

> Candlemas Day:
> Throw beans in the clay,
> Put candles and candlesticks all away.

St Valentine's Day: 14 February

Romans celebrated the fertility festival of Lupercalia on 14 February, which included young people drawing lots to choose their partner for the day, a custom found in England in the seventeenth century, when the man gave his partner a gift such as gloves. Valentine cards became popular in the early nineteenth century but country people Improvised 'cards': Sheila Stewart recorded in *Country Courtship* that they could be made from the discarded sole of a shoe, labelled 'You are a good old sole' or a shrivelled pig's tail labelled 'You are THE END'.

Several times a year, particularly after enclosure which gave agricultural labourers fewer opportunities to earn extra money, poor children came round reciting rhymes, which varied from village to village, to earn a few pennies, and Valentine's Day was no exception. Bodicote children recited:

> The rose is red, the violet's blue
> Carnation's sweet and so be you,
> So plaze to give us a Wolentine.

If they received something they were duly grateful, but if they were refused the rhyme was chanted again, changing the second line to:

> The Devil's black and so be you!

The Milton rhyme ran:

> I choose you if its not too late,
> If 'tis too late what shall I do?
> I hope it's not too late,
> For I have come to have an egg or two.

Valentining in Chipping Norton was unique: until the 1950s children congregated before school and went up and down the street visiting each shop, chanting:

I'll be yours if you'll be mine,
Please to give me your Valentine.

At most shops they received a shower of hot pennies, but Pettifer's the bakers gave them stale buns.

Shrove Tuesday and Lent

Shrove Tuesday was a day of celebration before the privations of Lent. People worked until 11.00 a.m. when the Pancake Bell was rung and men went home to eat pancakes. These were a practical way of finishing up milk and eggs which were forbidden during Lent. Before the Reformation people confessed their sins, after it they might pay to ring the church bells, throw at cocks, wrestle or play ball games during the afternoon.

The children went round with rhymes, often asking for food, such as this sung in the Baldons in 1895:

Pit-a-pat, the pan's hot,
I be come a Shroving,
Catch a fish afore the net,
That's better than nothing.
Eggs, lard and flour's dear,
This makes me come a-Shroving here.

If this did not produce the desired effect they continued:

Pit-a-pat, the pan's hot,
I be come a Shroving,
A bit of bread and a bit of cheese,
That's better than nothing.
For eggs, lard and flour's dear,
So I be come a Shroving here.

At the end of the Middle Ages consumption of meat, cheese and eggs was prohibited during Lent as were marriage and sexual intercourse. Sacred images in churches were veiled; the chancel was hidden from the congregation. On Ash Wednesday until 1548 ashes were blessed and sprinkled with holy water and dabbed on each person's forehead.

Lent Sundays were known as Tid (from the Te Deum), Mid (Mid Deus), Miserae (Miserere Mei), Carling or Care Sunday (from grey carling peas eaten that day, Care indicating anxiety before the Crucifixion), Palm or Passion Sunday was named after the palms distributed and Paste Egg day was Easter Sunday. Mid-Lent Sunday is Mothering Sunday, when people from outlying churches processed to their mother church, and the Lenten fast was relaxed for the day. Waffles were a common treat and maidservants, who had the day off, brought primroses, violets and simnel cake home as presents. It was a day for ball games at Chalgrove. Recently it has become linked with the American Mother's Day, instituted in 1913.

On Palm Sunday people processed carrying palm crosses and the branches were kept to protect the house while today palm crosses are distributed in church. Often figs were eaten, cooked and uncooked and baked into pies and puddings.

When children broke up for the Easter holidays they went from house to house rattling clacks of wood and reciting rhymes such as this Bletchingdon one, recorded in John Aubrey's seventeenth-century *MS Lansdowne*:

> Herrings, herrings, white and red,
> Ten a penny, Lent's dead;
> Rise, dame, and give an egg,
> Or else a piece of bacon.
> One for Peter, two for Paul,
> Three for Jack-a-Lent's all.
> Away, Lent, away.

When they received eggs or bacon they responded:

> Here sits a good wife,
> Pray God save her life;
> Sit her upon a hod
> And drive her to God.

If they received nothing they retorted:

> Here sits a bad wife,
> The Devil take her life;
> Set her upon a swivel
> And send her to the Devil.

Good Friday is the most solemn day in the ecclesiastical calendar and certain standards of behaviour were expected – it was taboo to do your washing that day, shoe a horse or do housework. Many people had the day off and primrosing was popular.

Easter

Country people rose early, hoping to see the sun jump for joy three times as it rose above the horizon, in thanksgiving for the Resurrection, and wore something new, believing that otherwise birds would make droppings on them. Easter eggs were often dyed in onion skins, or boiled in coloured water. Egg rolling took place on steep hillsides such as Shotover near Oxford. At Witney a puppet play depicting the Easter story was performed at Easter in the sixteenth century. Easter cake was baked for the Kidlington churchwardens to distribute to parishioners and apples were thrown at Northmoor. At Radley 'clipping the church', where the choir and parishioners joined hands round the building forming a large ring

and walking round, was revived in 1965. Ball games were popular on Easter
Monday and at Ascott-under-Wychwood and Chilson watercress teas were held.

Hock Monday and Tuesday

On Hock Monday and Tuesday, two weeks after Easter, until the seventeenth
century men and women raised money for the church by taking turns at 'lifting'
members of the opposite sex and 'ransoming' them. There are references to this in
the Henley-on-Thames churchwardens' accounts as early as 1457 and in Oxford
in the sixteenth century.

April Fool

April fool may date back to when the New Year began on 25 March and 1 April
was the last of eight days of celebration in Europe. Tricks were usually verbal such
as sending someone to buy pigeon's milk. Mollie Harris greeted tricksters who
tried jokes after twelve noon with:

> April Fool's Day's past,
> And you're the April Fool at last.

Inspecting the City Walls

When William of Wykeham built New College in 1379 he incorporated a section of the Oxford city wall, which since then has been inspected triennially by
the City Council, usually in the persons of the Chief Constable, Mayor, Sheriff,
Town Clerk, aldermen and councillors in official robes.

Riding the Franchise

The Mayor of Oxford 'rides the franchise' round the boundaries of the city, which
familiarises him with the area and enables councillors of newly incorporated areas
to meet their colleagues. In Victorian times the riding was often accompanied by
a military band or the City Waits. Each boundary stone was marked by having
the city mace and a flag placed on it, and refreshments were provided at intervals.
Now the boundary is so large, the Riding is often confined to new areas being
included: in 1991 the Mayor, Alan Pope, 'rode' round Littlemore, Old Marston,
Risinghurst and Sandhills, by boat, bus and on foot.

May Day

Celebrations on the first of May, marking the beginning of summer, have often
been lively: in 1250 the Chancellor of the University of Oxford forbade people

from wearing masks and making disorderly noises in churches or wearing greenery in processions. Garlands and green boughs were placed in churches and boys blew cows' horns or hollow canes at dawn. Adults gathered hawthorn boughs overnight to deck their doors for good luck, but this was stopped by Puritans' disapproval of potential lewd behaviour. Tall maypoles, decorated with ribbons and flowers, were erected, around which people performed ring dances, (but did not plait the ribbons as they do on the shorter maypoles introduced in the late nineteenth century). People were so passionate about May festivities that there were court cases over Puritan destruction of maypoles in Banbury in 1589 and 1590. May celebrations were banned under the Commonwealth and restored in 1660 by Charles II but during the eighteenth century fewer adults participated. May Games were celebrated at Combe, with a Lord and Lady, in the style of Whitsun Ales.

In Oxford the Sweeps' Procession was part of May Day, probably starting in the eighteenth century and continuing until about the First World War. May marked the end of the chimney-sweeping season, so sweeps went round in procession to earn a few extra pennies, singing:

> Please to remember the chimney-sweeps,
> Please kind Sir, don't pass us by,
> We're old sweeps, and want a living,
> Spare us a copper, as in olden time.

The May Morning Sweep's Procession, photographed by Henry Taunt in the 1890s. Two sweeps are dressed as the Lord and Lady (the latter in drag), accompanied by Jack-in-the-Green in a wicker costume decorated with evergreens and flowers, a Fool, men carrying shovels and pokers as musical instruments and men with money boxes.

During the nineteenth century May Day was taken over by the children, girls in particular, who made garlands which they carried round, reciting or singing rhymes and begging for pennies. Each village had its own May rhymes, some very similar. In the Bartons they sang:

> Gentlemen and Ladies,
> We wish you a happy May.
> We've come to show our Garland
> Because it is May Day.
> This garland we have brought,
> And at your door it stands.
> Tis but a sprout, but it is well put out
> With the work of Our Lord's hands.

It was believed that singing outside each door brought good luck and fertility to the household. From the 1870s May Day was often taken over by schools, who organised processions round villages led by the May King and Queen and their entourage of children who sang songs at each door and collected money, usually for a school tea. In Oxfordshire garlands were either crossed hoops or a pyramid shape, often with a doll in the centre, sometimes hidden by a veil which was lifted to earn pennies. Another way of earning pennies, especially at the back door of great houses where the servants congregated, was for the king to lift the queen's veil and give her a kiss.

May Day at Iffley, photographed by Henry Taunt in the 1890s. The Queen wears a veil and the King has smart epaulettes. The central garland contains a doll, and one of the others is made from two crossed hoops. The children, although probably dressed in their best, are obviously not well off.

May Day at Iffley about ten years later, photographed by Henry Taunt. This time the celebration has been taken over by the better off: the May Queen has a special white dress, she and the King wear garden foliage and lilies and the other children are well dressed. The boys with floral staves are 'policemen'. The principal garland is now a pyramid shape.

May Day celebrations at Charlton-on-Otmoor are unique in Oxfordshire: it is said that the church had fine statues of the Virgin Mary, the dead Christ and St John the Evangelist on the rood screen which were destroyed at the Reformation. The parishioners were horrified, but knew that if they replaced them they would be broken again, so they created frameworks for St John and the Virgin which they decorated with fresh evergreens for May Day and the men carried 'St John' and the women 'The Virgin' in procession round Otmoor, until about 1860, accompanied by morris men, enjoying a feast at Studley Priory, then putting the figures back on the rood screen.

Some schools still elect a May Queen and have maypole dancing. Such celebrations were particularly popular towards the end of the twentieth century as many schools marked their centenaries.

Oak Apple Day: 29 May

Charles II celebrated his birthday and his Restoration to the throne in 1660 on 29 May, so the day became associated with oak leaves and oak apples, and decorating doors with oak boughs, to commemorate his escape after defeat at the Battle of Worcester in 1651 when he hid in an oak tree. In the nineteenth century those who failed to wear oak apples in a gesture of loyalty to the Crown were pinched by their fellows. Oak was only worn until noon, and those found wearing it later were liable to be stung with stinging nettles. The day was also known as 'Shick-shack day'. The rhyme recited at Over Norton was:

May Day at Blackthorn in 1955. Children parade around Blackthorn and Ambrosden with their pyramid-shaped garland carried on broom handles and a collecting box.

The earliest illustration of the garlands, made from wicker decorated with evergreens which represent the Virgin Mary and St John the Evangelist, in Chariton-on-Otmoor church from Dunkin's *History and Antiquities of the Hundred of Bullingdon and Ploughley* (1823). Now only the figure of the Virgin is decorated.

The children of Chariton-on-Otmoor Primary School carry a long swagged garland of evergreens with bosses of flowers in procession to the church to hang across the rood screen. Other children carry small crosses decorated with flowers to place below the rood screen and on the church windowsills. A special service is held, followed by maypole dancing.

Oak apple day, 29th of May,
If you don't give us a holiday,
We'll all run away.

Robin Hood Games

In May and at Whitsun in the fifteenth and sixteenth centuries summer kings and queens were elected, called King of the May, Whitsun King, Summer Lord or Robin Hood and Maid Marion while other characters included Friar Tuck and Little John. Records found in Churchwardens' Accounts such as those of Henley-on-Thames, Thame and St Helen's church in Abingdon, indicate that they raised money for the church. A Robin Hood play was performed at Enstone as late as 1652 and in Bloxham it may have survived until the nineteenth century. Robin Hood games involved dancing, feasting and drinking and often a ritual fight between winter and spring. Elements of Robin Hood games have been preserved in Whitsun Ales.

Whitsun Ales

Churchwardens brewed ale to sell at Whitsun Ales, the proceeds of which went to the church. However Puritans disapproved because it encouraged drunkenness, as the more one drank, the more one supported the church. This disapproval resurfaced in the nineteenth century, leading to their decline. Whitsun was one of the main agricultural holidays and ales were an important source of entertainment.

Thomas Little visited the Woodstock Ale in 1826 and wrote in *Confessions of an Oxonian* that he was drawn by the sounds of singing, dancing, merriment and music provided by tabors, flutes, pipes, tambourines and fiddles. He was approached by a Fool in motley who asked him what he would call a painted wooden horse placed in a ring and when Little called it 'a wooden horse' he was informed that he would have to pay a forfeit of a shilling for miscalling it. On refusing, he was bundled onto the wooden horse, 'his lordship's gelding' behind an ugly red haired girl, so he rapidly changed his mind and paid the fine. Then he was accosted by one of her ladyship's maids of honour who pointed out a stuffed owl in a cage above the entrance to the bower, so he said it was the handsomest owl he had ever seen. The girl screeched and demanded a forfeit, and on his refusal called for 'her ladyship's cook' shouting that Little wished to marry her. Out came a girl with her face reddened with brick dust, carrying a toasting fork and a dishclout, ready to give her 'groom' three pricks with the toasting fork on each buttock during the mock ceremony, but he again paid his forfeit, and he was informed that he should have called the owl 'her ladyship's canary bird'.

There were many ales elsewhere, most with the same burlesque features. At Bicester a Lord and Lady and their retinue were chosen and morris dancers joined the festivities. The barn doors were decorated with an owl and a monkey, entitled 'my lord's parrot' and 'my lady's lap dog', and again forfeits were demanded from those who could not name them correctly. Maypoles often formed part of the festivities; the one at Blewbury was said to have been stolen from a nearby village. Some places such as Wantage and Wheatley held Whitsun sports such as cock-fighting instead of ales.

The Woodstock Whitsun Ale of 1826 showing 'Her Ladyship's Canary Bird' (the owl in the cage).
(From Percy Manning's *Stray Notes on Oxfordshire Folklore, Folklore*, vol. XIV, 1903)

Several factors, including the antipathy to drunkenness and the fact that many agricultural labourers became employed on a wage basis so could not afford many days off, contributed to the decline of the ales and their place was taken by the rise of the Friendly Societies which provided basic insurance for labouring classes.

Lord and Lady Lindsay of Lockinge House revived the idea of Whit Ales to hold an Elizabethan Revel on 26 and 27 August 1885. They and their guests wore Elizabethan dress; 'Mye Ladye's Reception Tent' was lined with silver, other marquees were erected for dancing and dining, the former lined with red and lit by chandeliers. Events began with a procession led by jesters and the revel banners, the Summer Queen in a carriage drawn by four oxen decorated with rose wreaths and gilded hooves, Robin Hood, Lord and Lady Wantage, morris and ribbon dancers, Yeomen halberdiers, heralds, pages, flower children, dancers, choirs and the band of the 1st Berks Regiment of Volunteers and the Ardington band. Robin Hood and his men performed, followed by quintain, a tournament, ribbon dancing and a mock bullfight with a pantomime bull. Wayland Smith made a surprise appearance and magically conjured up a living 'statue' of King Alfred. The next day the revels continued, perhaps with more of the flavour of a Whit Ale, as some of the 'lower order' managed to get in and it became too riotous for some of the more genteel!

Wychwood Forest Whit Hunt

Wychwood was a royal hunting forest which covered much of West Oxfordshire where only the king and a favoured few nobles were permitted to hunt, but on Whit Monday a special hunt was organised for the villagers of Brize Norton, Charlbury, Crawley, Ducklington, Finstock, Hailey and Leafield and townsfolk of Witney, Bampton and at one time Burford. They were summoned to hunt by the blowing of willow bark horns, where, accompanied by the king's huntsman, they hunted for three deer, one for Hailey, one for Crawley and one for Witney. The man first in at the death kept the antlers, and when the carcases were skinned everyone tried to obtain a piece of skin to wear in the cap for luck. The venison was cooked and shared by the community. Those not participating in the hunt danced round a maypole set up on the green and were entertained by morris dancers and decorated a bowery with green leaves ready for the feast. Burford suffered from plague in 1593 so lost its right to hunt in the forest for fear of infection and instead received two bucks annually. The hunt ceased when Wychwood was disafforested in the mid-nineteenth century.

Trinity Sunday and Lamb Ales

Lamb Ales took place around Trinity; definitely at Kirtlington and possibly also at Kidlington (although the only reference to this may be a misprint for Kirtlington). The reference to Kidlington was in T. Blount in *Ancient Tenures* (1679):

> At Kidlington … Monday after Whitson week, there is a fat lamb provided, and
> the Maids of the Town having their thumbs ty'd behind them, run after it, and she

Left: A 'peeling horn' made from twisted willow bark, held together with thorns with a reed in one end, made to summon men to the Whit Hunt near Witney in the early nineteenth century, preserved in the Pitt Rivers Museum, University of Oxford. (Photograph ref. PR100H)

Below: Illustration of the Lady from the Kirtlington Lamb Ale with her floral mace and a morris dancer with a pile of crown cakes, about 9in in diameter made from minced meat and batter in a rich currant and plum dough, which were considered luck-bringers and sold for half a crown each.

that with her mouth takes and holds the Lamb is declared Lady of the Lamb, which being dress'd with the skin hanging on, is carried on a long Pole before the Lady and her Companions on the Green, attended with Music and a Morisco Dance of Men, and another of women, where the rest of the day is spent in dancing with mirth and merry glee.

   The next day the Lamb is part bak'd, boyl'd, and roast, for the Ladies feast, where she sits majestically as the upper end of the Table, and her Companions with her with music and other attendants, which ends the solemnity.

The festivities expanded to last a week and at Kirtlington the Lady, a girl of good character, was paid a fee of twenty five shillings. The Lord came to the Lady's house to collect her on the Monday, Tuesday and Wednesday mornings and they processed to the Bowery, carrying floral maces, accompanied by morris dancers and a Fool. Although refreshments were free, donations were requested. On Wednesday a lamb was made into lamb pies including the 'head pie' which contained the complete head, including wool, which was sold for a shilling. The rest of the week was spent in feasting, drinking and dancing. After 1858 the Lamb Ale was replaced by the club feast of the Oddfellows and Box Club Friendly Societies. The Ale was revived in 1979 by the Kirtlington Morris Men who organise a weekend of dancing with teams from all over the country. They parade to a church service, dance round the Lady of the Lamb and tour local pubs. The Eynsham Lamb Ale died out in the early nineteenth century.

Club Feasts

The Clubs and Friendly Societies held annual feasts for their members who progressed to church for a service, then had a feast, often followed by dancing. The Filkins feast consisted of roast beef, ham and mutton with vegetables, plum puddings and jellies with beer and pop to drink. At Headington Quarry the rural sports and games which were part of the festivities included climbing a greasy pole to win a leg of mutton, men with hands tied behind them trying to catch cocks with their teeth and grinning through horse collars.

Midsummer: the Burford Dragon

Dr Plot was the first to describe the Burford Dragon ceremony in *History of Oxfordshire* (1677), where he claimed that the procession of a dragon and a picture of a giant through the town on Midsummer Eve commemorated a battle fought around AD 750 between Saxon kings Cuthred or Cuthbert and Ethelbald, the latter being defeated and his golden dragon banner captured. It is more likely that the dragon and giant are connected with the Merchant Tailors' Guild, as Burford's wealth came from wool and St John the Baptist, whose feast day is 24 June, was patron saint of the Guild. The dragon ceremony ceased in 1796 but was revived in 1971 by Burford School and now takes place annually.

The annual procession of the Bicester Order of the Ancient Court of Foresters, established in 1874, marching down Field Street to the music of the Bicester Band, c. 1906.

The Burford dragon ceremony was revived in 1971 by Burford School and now takes place annually. The dragon, giant and Gloucester City Morris Men parade down the hill from the school, stop at Burford church for a service, then the morris men dance.

In 1971 only one giant was made, but now several are sometimes found. This giant paraded in 1975.

Mock Mayors

Mock-mayormaking takes place where a new area has been added on to a town, such as Newland, built on the outskirts of Banbury as a new town in the twelfth century, but outside the borough boundary so its inhabitants were not entitled to vote. The mock mayor was a figure of fun elected in comic opposition to the real mayor. The Newland mock mayor was chaired around carrying a large cabbage stalk as a mace and accompanied by much drinking. The last mock-mayormaking was around 1860.

Old Headington was a small village, so it is a mystery why a mock mayor was elected, but he was chaired round the village in a bower of evergreens on the Wednesday of Whitsun week. In Oxford the Lower Freemen of the city chose a mayor of 'Sloven's Court' (which became corrupted to 'Sclavonian'). The court had to detect any non-freeman, (who were not entitled to vote) present in the Town Hall and offenders were brought before the Lord of the Court, who wore mock-regal costume, and fined, or if they refused to pay had a bucket of cold water poured down their sleeves.

Old Woodstock was founded by Henry I when he enlarged Woodstock Park, and remained part of Wootton parish until 1887, while the town of Woodstock dates from the reign of Henry II, who wanted services for his court when he stayed at Woodstock Palace. Mock-mayormaking began before 1786, the date on the wooden mace. It used to take place in September and was accompanied by a cricket match and dinner at the Rose and Crown, the mayor often being chosen for his drinking capacity. It lapsed in the 1920s and was revived in 1954, when a robe was made for the mayor from a red blanket, worn with a chain of office made from curtain rings and a top hat. The original mace disappeared for a time so a new one was made from a holly stick entwined with a large cabbage stem topped by a coronet. Each candidate stands on an upturned beer can to say what he or she can offer to Woodstock. In 1993 one candidate proposed to bring the Olympic Games to Blenheim Park, while the winner, Edward Saxton, said he had booked good weather for the following year's performance, as that year it had been postponed because of rain. Then the committee went into the pub to deliberate and onlookers were told to look for the white smoke (the signal that a new pope has been chosen). The mock mayor processed down the hill from the Rose and Crown to swim across the River Glyme, then the company went back up the hill to drink the evening away. Now the Rose and Crown has closed and the Black Prince is used instead.

Fairs

Fairs played an important role in the economic life of towns and goods were sold there which were unobtainable at other times of year. Autumn fairs had a hiring section where labourers, wearing tokens of their occupations, such as a piece of whipcord in the pocket of a carter, stood in line and had interviews with prospective employers. If the pair came to an agreement, the farmer would give the man a shilling and told him to turn up for work the following Monday. Many towns held a second 'runaway mop' fair about a month later which gave further job opportunities.

At the 1993 Woodstock mock-mayormaking, when there was controversy as to whether or not Woodstock should have a bypass, one candidate, Mel Williams, promised that if he became Mayor he would tax vehicles according to the number of wheels they had, then he rode off on a unicycle.

Many towns held several fairs a year, each specialising in a different commodity, such as horses, cows, sheep or cheese. Deddington had a Pudding Pie Fair in November, where sheep, pigs and cattle were sold and there were many stalls.

Fairs provided rare organised entertainment; people thought nothing of walking ten or twenty miles to visit them and with the advent of the railways came from further away. As the commercial aspect of fairs declined, the pleasure aspect increased. George Herbert described a camera obscura at an early nineteenth-century Banbury Fair while in 1910 it boasted Gage's Boxing Booth, Alf Ball's Wild West Show, a Biascope, steam yachts and side shows.

Ironically St Giles Fair, the sole remaining one in Oxford, is not a fair granted by the town's charter and originated as Walton Wakes in Walton Manor, outside the city boundary. *Jackson's Oxford Journal* of 10 September 1887 reported that the goods on offer included: 'baskets, glass and china ornaments, cheap tools, sweets, gingerbread, cakes etc, while there were scores of barrows on which were fruit … cocoa nuts, hedge nuts, cheap jewellery, photographs, ices, canaries and other cage birds. braces, gilding fluid, potato peelers, name stamps, and other things too numerous to mention.' The novelty items were like a mini 'Great Exhibition' from clockwork humming birds to incubators.

Entertainments were kept up-to-date: during Wantage Fair in 1833 barmaid Ann Pullin was murdered in the Red Lion by a customer, and George Sanger, who witnessed her decapitation, sat up all night with his father to recreate the scene in a peep show, which proved very popular the next day. Witney Feast is believed to be over 750 years old, originating in a festival commemorating the dedication of the church. Entertainments in the 1860s included Singer's Royal Wax Works exhibition, Mr Moreland's Theatricals, cosmoramical exhibitions and learned pigs.

Entertainments in the late nineteenth century at St Giles Fair in Oxford, photographed here in 1909, included elaborate roundabouts, a trapeze railway and in 1895 a Channel Tunnel railway.

Wakes

Parishes held feasts to commemorate their patronal festivals, mostly grouped around Whitsun or from August to November. By the eighteenth century they had a secular character, with drinking and feasting and often small fairground type entertainments such as roundabouts and swingboats. All dressed in their best clothes and the village would be packed with people. At Uffington the feast was combined with sports such as wrestling and backswording.

Halloween and Guy Fawkes Night

Halloween was the feast of the dead, when it was believed that the gap between our world and the spirit world was at its narrowest, so ghosts walked and witches held covens and turnip or pumpkin heads with candles inside were made to frighten away ghosts.

It was a time for bonfires, but when James I escaped being blown up in the Houses of Parliament bonfires were lit to celebrate, and since then they have been lit on 5 November instead of Halloween. Usually an effigy of Guy Fawkes, one of the plotters, was burnt, but over the years other unpopular characters have been guys such as the Kaiser during the First World War and once an unpopular Oxford alderman.

November 5th was notorious for riotous behaviour with gangs of boys going round demanding wood for their bonfires, chanting rhymes such as this Headington one:

> Remember, remember,
> The fifth of November
> Bonfire night,
> We want a faggot
> To make it alight.
> Hatchetts and ducketts,
> Beetles and wedges,
> If you don't give us some,
> We'll pull your old hedges,
> If you won't give us one,
> We'll take two,
> The better for us,
> And the worse for you.

In Burford tar barrels were rolled down the hill and in Witney they formed part of the fights between rival gangs, which often began as football matches. In Oxford there were violent fights between Town and Gown.

Christmas

Preparations for Christmas began with making the Christmas puddings, a family activity when everyone had a stir for good luck, before St Andrew's Day,

30 November, when the collect for the day contains the words 'Stir up, stir up, we beseech thee'.

Evergreens were put up on Christmas Eve and taken down by Twelfth Night. Children begged for apples for decorations with the rhyme:

> Holly and ivy, mistletoe bough,
> Give me an apple. And I'll go now,
> Give me another for my little brother,
> And I'll go home and tell father and mother.

John Aubrey wrote in 1686 that at Launton:

> ...it is ye custom for the Maid servant to ask the Man for Ivy to dress the House, and if the Man denies or neglects to fetch in the ivy, the Maid steals away a pair of his Breeches and nails them up to ye gate in the yard or highway.

This may reflect the belief that ivy represented woman and holly man. Christmas trees, although introduced to England from Germany in the eighteenth century, did not become popular until Queen Victoria and Prince Albert used them at Windsor Castle. Earlier kissing boughs, crossed hoops decorated with evergreens, apples and candles, were used. In Oxford a triad of lighted candles placed in a window on Christmas Eve indicated that any passer by was welcome to come inside for refreshment.

Wassailing was recorded in Henley-on-Thames in 1555, and in the nineteenth century, in the Vale of White Horse, wassailers carried a large wassail bowl from house to house, hoping it would be filled with Lambs' Wool, made from hot ale, sugar, spices, eggs and roasted apples, sometimes with cream and sippets of bread.

Carols date from the Middle Ages, when they were performed as ring dances, but many new ones were written in the nineteenth century which may have encouraged a revival in carol singing. In Adderbury in the 1830s and '40s waits, made up of working class men, went from house to house, with music provided by the village orchestra. At Swalcliffe carols sung by the waits included *While Shepherds Watched their Flocks by Night* and *Good King Wenceslas*. In the mid-nineteenth century carol singing began to be taken over by children, sometimes choirboys as at Iffley. Bell-ringing was often done on Christmas Eve.

Farmers rewarded their labourers by killing a bullock and giving each man a joint of beef, a rare luxury for them. Owners of big houses threw parties for the village children. Poor children hardly received any presents, although their Christmas stockings would contain an apple in the toe, nuts, dates and a few small toys and an orange. Families made their own entertainment, playing games such as Hunt the Slipper, Charades and Sardines.

Boxing Day

The holiday over the twelve days of Christmas became eroded in the nineteenth century, but some people could celebrate over several days. Boxing Day is dedicated to the two St Stephens, one of whom was patron saint of horses, who were supposed to be especially well treated that day. Boxing Day hunts were popular events.

Many churches distributed the contents of their poor boxes that day, and apprentices solicited tips from their masters' customers. Dunkin wrote in 1816 that the poor of Bicester gathered together to visit the gentry and tradesmen to ask for a Christmas box, expecting a penny for each adult and a half-penny per child.

In Bampton a St Stephen's breakfast was held before enclosure in 1812.

Abingdon Bun Throwing

This is in a slightly different category, as it takes place on special occasions rather than regularly. Bun throwing probably began in 1760 to mark the accession of George III, the first Hanoverian king born in England, or in 1761 at his coronation. Abingdon was then the county town of Berkshire, and it was customary to distribute loaves in the market place, and the idea was adapted for the councillors to hurl them from the roof of County Hall. It is usually performed to commemorate royal occasions such as coronations and weddings, and was done in 2000 to mark the 100th birthday of HRH Queen Elizabeth the Queen Mother. In 1820 1,000 buns were thrown for the coronation of George IV and 2,500 on Victory Day in 1946.

ten

MORRIS DANCING AND MUMMERS' PLAYS

Morris Dancing

There is a strong tradition of Cotswold morris dancing in Oxfordshire, which dates back several centuries. Morris dancing may have begun as a court entertainment around 1500, gradually filtering down to the villages. There are very early references from Thame and from Abingdon (which became part of Oxfordshire in the 1974 boundary changes) where in 1560 the churchwardens' accounts include the purchase of bells for the morris men, suggesting that they danced at money-raising events for the church such as church ales. Puritans condemned the dancing in the seventeenth century, but it revived at Charles II's Restoration in 1660, when there were sides at Bicester, Burford, Kirtlington and Somerton, with oral traditions of others at Abingdon and Bampton among others.

Most dancers in rural areas were agricultural labourers and the week of dancing around Whitsun gave a welcome boost to their incomes. In towns like Abingdon they had a variety of jobs reflecting the local economy such as railway porter, fellmonger, draper, weaver, horse dealer, baker and flax dresser. Some teams such as Kirtlington were fortunate to have a patron, often the lord of the manor, who ensured that they had sufficient meat to give them the stamina required for the dancing. The men usually began to practise about six weeks before their first performance of the year, often for an hour or so a day. Some teams such as Bampton were very close knit units, with much intermarriage between families, and their steps a closely guarded secret passed down from one generation to the next.

The teams were usually accompanied by a Fool, a Ragman who looked after the costumes, the treasurer who carried the money box and some teams, particularly in the Wychwood area, had a swordbearer who carried a cake impaled on his sword as a symbol of good luck and fertility. Morris costumes since the eighteenth century have usually consisted of white shirts, black or white breeches, ribbon baldricks and silk or beaver hats or caps, with light boots. Bells worn around the calves supplement the music provided by pipe and tabor, fiddle or concertina.

David Edgington, the Fool of the Bampton Morris Men in the 1890s. Usually the Fool carried a blown up bladder and pig's tail attached to a stick which he used to gently belabour the crowd to make a space for the men to dance and persuade them to give generously. As he was in charge of the money he had to keep his head and not get drunk.

Most information about morris dancing dates from the nineteenth century, although oral memories take some teams back further. Morris dancing declined with the decline of Whit Ales and other seasonal festivities which involved drinking, and in some places died out completely in the late nineteenth century. Cecil Sharp was so fascinated by seeing the Headington dancers perform on Boxing Day 1899 that he spent years studying and publishing material about morris dancing, which helped encourage a revival. The second half of the twentieth century saw another revival, with dancers coming from a wider background, including young professionals. Now several places such as Abingdon, Bampton and Adderbury boast more than one team, and the current interest is illustrated by the number of websites devoted to the subject. The best source of information for the history of local morris dancing up to 1900 is Keith Chandler's *Morris Dancing in the English South Midlands*.

Abingdon

Churchwardens' Accounts of St Helen's Church have early references to morris men from 1554-92, but the next information dates from the eighteenth century. Part of the regalia of the Abingdon Traditional Morris Men is a magnificent pair of ox horns, fought over by local residents in 1700 and won by the men of Ock Street. The 'Maid of the Mill' dance (which may depict the wheel of Ock Mill, with the mayor of Ock Street as the hub, and other dancers forming spokes

The Abingdon Morris Dancers performing 'The girl I left behind me' at the Abingdon Abbey grounds, c. 1937. The Abingdon style differs from the rest of Oxfordshire in having a distinctive regular beat, and dancers lift their legs high, stamp and use energetic arm movements.

Tom Hemmings chaired as mock mayor of Ock Street, Abingdon, in 1953. The musician is Major Francis Fryer and the boy, Stuart Jackson, became mayor himself in 1996. The Hemmings family proudly claim to have had members in the team over several centuries, and in 1978 Mr Hemmings' Traditional Abingdon Morris Dancers were formed, named after Tom Hemmings, by his grandson Brian Clark.

and iron rims as they dance) ends with dancers facing the musician and standard bearer and bowing to 'honour the horns'. The teams dance round local pubs over the summer, but the principal event for the Abingdon Traditional Morris Men is the election of the mock mayor of Ock Street, (which was outside the boundaries of Abingdon) held on the Saturday after 19 June. All residents of the street have the right to vote, and candidates usually have a connection with the morris men. Thomas Hemmings, who was born in 1815, claimed to have been mayor about twenty-five times. Today, after the poll has closed at 4.00 p.m. the votes are counted, and the real mayor of Abingdon is often asked to present the mock mayor with his traditional regalia: an applewood cup or mazer (said to have been carved from a club wielded by one of the Hemmings family in the 1700 fight), a sword and a sash. The mock mayor is carried shoulder high, in a flower-decked chair around Ock Street before returning to the Brewery Tap where an evening of dancing is held, including invited dancers from all over Britain. Traditionally the mock mayor visited and drank at all the pubs in Ock Street, but the Brewery Tap is the sole survivor.

'The Duke of Marlborough' is danced to the tune of a Danish cobbler's song probably learnt during campaigns with the Duke of Marlborough; other dances include 'The Squire's Dance', 'The Girl I left Behind Me', 'The 'Curly-Headed Ploughboy', 'Jockey to the Fair', 'Shepherd's Hey', 'The Berkshire Broom Dance', 'The Noble Duke of York' and 'The Nutting Girl'.

The Abingdon Morris Men dancing at the Woodstock mock-mayormaking in 1992.

Bampton

Oral tradition in Bampton claims that morris dancing has existed here for six hundred years, although it cannot definitely be taken back earlier than the eighteenth century. Whit Monday is a traditional day of dancing. In the nineteenth century Whit Monday was Bampton Club Feast Day and morris men processed round the town led by their musician, originally playing a whittle and dub, later a fiddle, then eight morris dancers with their Squire or Clown armed with his bladder and a sword-bearer with a cake (presented by the lady of the manor) and a bunch of flowers impaled on his sword. Anyone hoping to have a baby in the coming year would request a piece of the cake to bring fertility. Members of both Bampton clubs processed to church, accompanied by bands. Although club feasts have gone, the morris dancing continues, and children make garlands which they exhibit, hoping to earn a little money.

The Wells family had a long association with the morris, the most famous one being William 'Jinky' Wells, who gave much information to Cecil Sharp. He dressed in a clown outfit while the team wore costumes decorated with rosettes and wrist ribbons, a crimson sash and billycock hats decorated with real or artificial flowers. William Wells added several dances to the Bampton repertoire, often learned from musicians who played for other local teams.

'Constant Billy', the longest dance, could be performed in several different ways; there were eight six-handed side step dances: 'The Forester's Jig', 'The Bride in

The Bampton Morris Men dancing in Thame High Street in 1951, with Jinky Wells playing the fiddle.

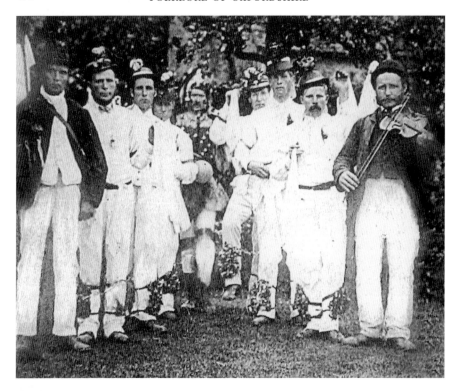

The Bampton Morris Men outside Bampton Manor in the 1890s. From left to right: Harry 'Sarah' Radband, George Wells, Joe Rouse, Jim 'Cocky' Tanner, David Edgington (the Fool), Philip 'Philly' Dew, George Dixey, Tom 'Buscot' Tanner, Dick Butler. The team has eight members although most dances are for six men.

Camp', 'The Nutting Girl', 'Old Tom of Oxford', 'The Quaker', 'Highland Mary', 'Johnny's so Long at the Fair' and 'Plum Pudding' which included the words:

> Lumps of plum pudding and pieces of pie,
> My mother she gave me for telling a lie.

They also perform clap dances 'Glorishears' and 'The Maid of the Mill', corner dances 'The Shepherd's Hey', 'The Rose Tree' and 'Banbury Bill', knee dance 'The Flowers of Edinburgh,' jigs 'The Webley', 'Princess Royal', 'The Fool's Jig', 'Jogging to the Fair', and 'The Pipe Dance'. They also danced country dances and had a processional dance entitled 'Bonny Green Garters' which began:

> My sister's going to Abingdon Fair,
> Bonny green garters I'm buying you each a pair...

Whit Monday is still a wonderful day to visit Bampton to watch the various teams perform.

Headington Quarry

Headington Quarry also proudly proclaims the length of its tradition. Villagers were mostly involved in seasonal work such as quarrying, brickmaking and hauling, which depended on good weather, so dancing helped provide extra money in lean times. The team progressed round local villages during Whit week from the 1870s, travelling to Wheatley, the Miltons and Long Crendon, returning to the Quarry to dance on Whit Monday at the feast of the Havelock Lodge of Oddfellows and at the Britannia Inn, Headington, and occasionally on request.

William Kimber's family had a long association with morris dancing, and he played the fiddle for Headington Quarry. He too became friendly with Cecil Sharp and provided him with much information. He was presented with a Gold Badge by the English Folk Dance and Song Society in 1922 and a street in New Headington was named after him following his death aged nearly ninety in 1961 where the team dance each spring bank holiday in his honour. Many boys used to be taught morris dancing at school.

Headington dances include 'Bean Setting' which imitates the task of dibbling beans into the earth, 'Rodney Drawback,' 'Blue-eyed Stranger', 'Double Setback', 'Laudanum Bunches', 'Constant Billy', 'Rigs o'Marlow,' 'Haste to the Wedding',

The Headington Quarry Morris Dancers performing a stick dance, c. 1899. William Kimber is playing the fiddle and the Fool is Sip Washington. The team disbanded around 1887 but Percy Manning of New College, who was collecting material on Oxfordshire customs and folklore, persuaded them to dance for him at the Corn Exchange in Oxford on 15 March 1899, which began their revival.

'the Old Woman Tossed up in a Blanket' and 'Old Mother Oxford' which includes the song:

> Old Mother Oxford's just come home,
> Had to light a fire in the big back room,
> Step and fetch her,
> Down the middle, down the middle,
> Step and fetch her, my pretty little dear,
> Don't you tease her, try to please her,
> 'Cause she is my pretty little dear.

Morris Sides

Teams were found throughout Oxfordshire, especially in the Wychwood Forest area at Ascott-under-Wychwood, Asthall Leigh, Burford, Churchill, Ducklington, Eynsham, Field Assarts, Finstock, Idbury, Kencot and Langford, Leafield, Milton-under-Wychwood, Minster Lovell, North Leigh, Spelsbury, Stanton Harcourt and Woodstock, many touring the local area during Whit week. In the 1840s the Ducklington team was made up solely from members of the Fisher family. At Eynsham the morris men came out to perform with the mummers. At Finstock the men danced on Holy Thursday as well at Whitsun. Spelsbury was unusual in having a team of women in addition to the men in the early nineteenth century, consisting of unmarried farmers' and labourers' daughters who danced on Spelsbury church tower to celebrate a victory, possibly in 1815 after the Battle of Waterloo.

The Eynsham Morris Dancers at Bampton Manor. Note the pheasant feathers decorating the hats.

At Adderbury three teams danced before 1860, each taking a different circuit during Whit week, but all attending Banbury Fair. For some years their fool was William Castle, known as 'Old Mettle' (*c.* 1789-1841), a matchseller considered a local figure of fun, who occasionally dressed in an old mortar board and gown, and was also fool for Bloxham morris.

A Bicester team danced at the Whit Ale of 1790. The Bucknell morris had patronage from Col. Hibbert of Bucknell Manor who offered the team a guinea if they returned from their week's tour as clean as when they had left, so they washed their clothes on the eve of their return.

The Kirtlington team was associated with the Lamb Ale, and as it received patronage from the Dashwood family of Kirtlington Park wore their colours of light blue and pink. The Wheatley dancers had a unique dance called the 'Wheatley Processional'.

Morris dancing is currently popular in Oxfordshire with thriving teams at Adderbury, Bloxham and Queen Emma's Morris of Ducklington (both female teams), the mixed Cattern team at Towersey, Charlbury, (which also has a children's team, the Cherries), Cry Havoc of Botley, Ducklington, Eynsham, Icknield Way of West Hendred, Kirtlington, North Moreton, North Leigh and Finstock, the Oxford City Morris Men and University Morris Men, Towersey and Wheatley as well as the stalwarts of Abingdon, Bampton and Headington Quarry.

Mummers' Plays

Mummers' plays, based on the hero combat theme of death and resurrection, are performed around the Christmas period. Characters such as St George and the Turkish knight, often the main protagonists, perhaps suggest a hark-back to medieval wars with the Turks, but the plays were not written down until the late eighteenth or early nineteenth century, although they may have been passed down from father to son in oral tradition before that. Over the years many speeches have become distorted, so current mummers often ad lib a great deal to reflect current interests, such as the Abingdon mummers on the eve of the first Gulf War referring to Saddam Hussein, and the Headington Quarry Mummers in 2002 referring to Cherie Blair buying flats in Bristol.

The plays have a swashbuckling hero, usually St George (or as he often became after George I's, accession to the throne, King George), but other heroes include King Alfred (in Wantage, Alfred's birthplace), the Royal Persian King (Sutton Courtenay), the Africky King (Steventon), King William (Long Wittenham), or the Royal Duke of Blunderland (Islip). He enters with a speech such as this one from Leafield:

> Oh I am the Royal of Prussia King,
> Born to defend all Christendom.
> We fought many a battle at home and abroad;
> That's all true upon my word:
> I fears no Spanish, French nor Turk,
> And there's no man can do me any hurt.
> So let all your noble voices ring.

The Headington Mummers in theatrical costumes with King George and the Turkish Knight or Turkey Snite, performing at the Chequers in Headington Quarry in 1901. Photographed by E.H. Binney.

> I am the Royal of Prussia King.
> I am the man just come from land.
> Where is the man that dare to bid me stand?
> I'll hack him and cut him down with my courageous hand
> I'll hack him and cut him as small as flies
> And send him to the Devil to make mince pies:
> Mince pies hot, mince pies cold,
> I'll send him to the Devil before he's nine days old.

The enemy was usually the Turkish Knight (or Turkey Snite as he was known in Headington Quarry) or Bold Slasher, but at the Bartons King George fought the Royal Prussian King, at Brightwell-cum-Sotwell the enemy was a Gay French Officer (gay in the old meaning of 'cheerful'). Other enemies included the Royal Prussia King, alias Starcher (Uffington), Tipton Slasher (Cholsey), Beau Slash (Drayton) and Bull Slasher (Sutton Courtenay). He defies the hero with words such as these from the Jolly Frenchman at Kirtlington:

> In comes I, the Jolly Frenchman.
> The Jolly Frenchman am I.
> Where is that man that bid me stand.
> Said he'd cut me up with his created hand.
> So am I'm come to face my foe,
> To give this man the created blow.
> So cock up your soord, and keep guard on yer eye,
> Else down in this house, you'll very soon lie.

In 2004 the Headington Mummers claimed to be sponsored by Allied Carpets so King George was careful to 'die' on a small piece of carpet. His 'chain mail' is a string vest painted silver. The mummers' contemporary references in 2004 were to 'fast-tracking visas' following the scandal when David Blunkett, the Home Secretary, was accused of helping his mistress's nanny.

The Headington Quarry Mummers' performance begins with their womenfolk ringing hand-bells, then after the play the morris men perform a sword dance. This was taught to the team by students from Yorkshire and Northumberland, and as it is not part of the Oxfordshire morris tradition is only performed at Christmas.

The Master of Ceremonies is usually Father Christmas, but sometimes Anno Domini (Islip), Beezlebub (Iffley and Lockinge), or the Announcer (Sunningwell). The hero and his opponent fight, one is killed, then the Doctor (who often wears a top hat and claims to be a Harley Street doctor) enters, who at Headington Quarry claims he can cure:

> All sorts of diseases, such as the hipsy, the pipsy, and the gout,
> Pains within and pains without.
> If the Devil's in him, I'll fetch him out.
> A touch on the heart and a touch on the knee,
> Rise up King George and follow me.

The Doctor's techniques have been updated to include birth control pills (Abingdon) and electric shock treatments with car batteries (Headington Quarry) to revive his patient. His patter can last several minutes.

Various other comic characters appear, who have now lost most of their words, so their meaning is uncertain. The man–woman figure (suggesting the days before 1660 when women were not allowed to perform on stage), is often known as Molly, Mary Tinker (Lockinge), Old Woman Ann (Sunningwell), or Mother Vinney (Uffington). Mr Finney, another character, is very proud of his status; at Burford a dragon and a giant feature (reflecting the characters in the midsummer procession), Beezlebub often appears, as does Bighead, at Souldern called Jack Pudding who says:

The Abingdon Mummers, who perform regularly at the Advent weekend at Manor Farm Cogges near Witney as well as in Abingdon, wear costumes made from white lab coats decorated with newspaper and different colours of crêpe paper to denote the different characters. The Turkish Knight is here played by Rod James who worked at the Oxfordshire County Museum, where his Jordanian colleague Ahmed Shistawi gave him Arabic newspapers to use on his costume.

Ear comes I, as never come yet,
With my gret head and my little wit;
My head is gret, my wit is small,
I'll do my dooty to plaze you all.

The earliest play recorded is from Islip, dating from 1780. The characters are Anno
Domini, the Royal Duke of Blunderland, Earl or King Percy, Herald, Pedlar Knave,
Quack Doctor Spinney, Salt Peter, Old Fat Jack and Old Father Christmas.

Some mummers wore 'paper costumes', attaching strips of paper to smocks or
shirts. In Long Hanborough mummers toured the village before Christmas asking for old newspapers for their costumes. Sometimes identities were disguised
by strips of paper over the face, and sometimes faces were blackened. Sometimes
more theatrical elements were added such as a paper coronet for the Duke of
Thumberland at Brightwell-cum-Sotwell.

There are many local variants of mummers' plays. Some were derived from
chapbooks, given local variations. A Christmas Robin Hood play performed at
Shipton-under-Wychwood was adapted from the ballad of 'Robin Hood and the
Tinker'. Plays were performed in streets or public houses, or in private houses, and
performers often created their own space for the action by walking round in a circle.

Mumming faded in the late nineteenth or early twentieth century, with reviv-
als such as the one in Headington Quarry in the 1930s when the text of their play
was published. Today several mummers' plays are performed, largely connected

The Bampton Mummers in 1946. From left to right: Ted Hunt, Bill Daniels, Robert Radband, Terry Rouse,
Barry Taylor. A play was written specially for the Bampton Mummers in 1847 by local historian Dr Giles.

with morris sides. Plays are currently performed at Adderbury (where, unusually, women take some of the parts), Abingdon, Bampton, Blewbury, Charlbury, Chinnor, Drayton, Ducklington, Faringdon, Finstock, Headington Quarry, Wantage and Witney. The plays are performed with great gusto, and form a tradition which is well worth supporting.

eleven

The Supernatural

Fairies

A strong belief in fairies is illustrated in the writing of plays by William Shakespeare and John Milton, both of whom knew this area, in the sixteenth and seventeenth centuries. Milton described goblins, pinching fairies, the will-o'-the-wisp, circles of tiny elves and lucky fairies who visited a house when a baby was born.

Recently fairies have been seen at the Rollright Stones by an old man who described them as 'little folk like girls to look at', while his widow said that they came out of a bank near the King Stone, and that she and her friends placed a stone over the hole to stop them coming out, but the stone had moved the next morning, although they may have found a rabbit hole or similar! In 1976 Christina Hole was told that people who led a pure life could see fairies near the Whispering Knights.

In the woods near Stoke Row there is a distorted old tree trunk which always contains a pool of water, and in the early twentieth century it was said that fairies drove there on Midsummer Eve in coaches and their horses drank from the pool. J.H. Baker recorded in *The Story of the Chiltern Hundreds* that at Nuney Green there was a pond 'surely where the "Little People", the sprites and gnomes of the woodlands, come to fill their pails at night in the moonlight.'

Adwell Cop near Thame has a Bronze Age barrow, which local people associated with the fairies; such barrows have often been thought to be entrances into the fairy world. The eighteenth-century antiquary, Delafield, recorded the story of a traveller who saw them dancing on the Cop and singing:

> At Adwell Cop there stands a cup.
> Drink the drink and eat the sop
> And set the cup on Adwell Cop.

Marshy areas often emit a phosphorescent gas, which can explode at certain temperatures, sometimes known as *ignis fatuus* or as corpse lights, and it is probably this which has given rise to legends of the will-o'-the-wisp or jack-o'-lantern seen at Fringford Mill and Middle Aston Mill. Miss Drake who lived at Fringford Mill as a child recalled that her mother was once misled by 'corpse lights' and nearly fell into a backwater of the mill stream. The red lights resembled little gnomes about three feet high, who looked as though their lower legs were concealed in the grass. They bobbed up and down emitting a singing sound, coming to within a foot or so of a human, then bobbing away again. In about 1970 two girls were run over by a car when they were seduced by the lights off the grass verge near Fringford Mill. A shire horse kept in a nearby field where corpse lights appeared always trembled with fear when going through the gate. The lights were very much in evidence in 1918 when many people died in Fringford from influenza. They also appear in foggy weather in the early winter. A strange light, looking like a man carrying a lantern, nicknamed Jinny Burn Tail, used to be seen near Ascott-under-Wychwood.

Katharine Briggs in *The Folklore of the Cotswolds* recorded a story told by an Oxfordshire farmer about a lazy, hard-drinking labourer, who was always the first to swig from the firkin provided by the farmer at harvest, even when he was sent to work in the middle of the field. He once ran off with the firkin and, already quite drunk, lay on a mound with a hawthorn on it. Suddenly he saw small green creatures round the bank, and became temporarily paralysed. As soon as he could move again he rose, took another swig and muttered, 'What a funny dream I had … all about nothing.' Tiny voices twittered back 'And that's what you'll find in the firkin'.

Ruth Tongue recorded an Oxfordshire fairy story about True John and Greedy Jack. True John, an old man, had a fruit tree which was the envy of the neighbourhood, but he only charged a penny a pound for the fruit and nobody was allowed to buy more than three pounds, because he said that he 'and his helpers' wanted the poor to share it. There were always crowds of small birds around the tree, and at night hundreds of little lights bobbing around it, accompanied by sweet singing and wonderful perfume from the blossom.

Greedy Jack, the farmer, had fine fruit trees, but no lights or singing, and he shot at any birds that came near them. He once shot at True John's tree and the green birds pecked at the eyes of Jack and his men so they fled, and his men never returned to work for him. After he had bathed his sore eyes in the stream Jack returned home and saw that his fruit has been hit by shot and fallen to the ground, whereas True John's tree was as fine as ever. Greedy Jack never prospered again, but when True John died he bought his cottage, and chopped down the fruit tree in spite, hoping that the lights would move to his trees. However that night a weird wind demolished all his trees and the voices from the dancing lights twittered: 'True John is gone, gone, gone!' All but one light disappeared and a voice wailed: 'Greedy Jack, Greedy Jack, We shall never come back'.

Witchcraft

Witches were feared in the Roman era, and witchcraft may have its origins in prehistoric religious beliefs. During the persecution of witches in the sixteenth and seventeenth centuries many old women who were guilty of nothing more than having a sharp tongue and a deep knowledge of herbal medicine appear to have been branded witches. Witchcraft has often been associated with mystical prehistoric sites such as the Rollright Stones (where pagan ceremonies are held today) and Wayland's Smithy.

In the Churchwarden's Presentments of 1520 a certain Letys Dorham of Watlington was said 'to make use of witchcraft'. During the reign of Charles I a woman was condemned and executed after being charged with riding through the air on a bed staff and teaching her seven-year-old child to fly. In the early seventeenth century Anne Gunther was seized with fits and local women believed she was a witch, so she was questioned by Oxford scholars and an expert in sorcery from Newbury. When Anne sneezed pins came out of her body, her eyes bulged, she foamed at the mouth and her body swelled and contracted. She claimed to see local women Agnes Pepplewell as a white mouse and Elizabeth Gregory as a black rat with a pig's head and both were tried and detained at Abingdon; Anne herself was brought before James I in London three times and tried in the Star Chamber.

In the Calendar of Oxfordshire Quarter Sessions Joanna Walker of Burcester (Bicester) petitioned in 1687 against a false accusation of witchcraft and in 1723 Sarah Lockton was assaulted by Elizabeth Horne who believed her to be a witch.

James Jagger was an eighteenth-century cunning man from Bicester, an illegitimate boy brought up by George Gurden at the turnpike house. In 1793 he tried to raise the Devil, who apparently appeared, only to disappear in a clap of thunder. Jagger won a reputation for finding lost goods and detecting thieves so Mrs Saunders, licencee of the Rose and Crown, asked him to find her lost silver clasp. Jagger set a tub of water in the passage, then performed rites and evocations in a nearby room. The clasp splashed into the water when Jagger was nowhere near. On his way home he was about to unlock his door when he was whisked over the tops of the trees by an invisible force, dragged through hedges, ditches and ponds until he was found next morning four miles away at Kirtlington Bottom, claiming that he had been attacked by demons resembling asses with panniers on their backs.

Miriam Russell terrorised Barton near Headington in the early nineteenth century, riding around on a dough cover (the lid of a wooden trough for kneading dough). She once requested something from Stowford Farm, Barton and on being refused issued threats. A few days later cows and calves ran around as though mad and some calves were found on the roof of the thatched barn. When Miriam claimed this as her work the Powells who owned the farm gave her all she required and the animals returned to normal.

Betty Cam lived in Stanton St John in the mid-nineteenth century. She was said to ride around on hurdles, frighten cattle, lame horses and break wagons, but she could be helpful: once Mr Snow saw Betty was in a service tree and she filled his hat with berries. Betty had an uncanny knowledge of the activities of the youngsters, so one day a gang went to punish her for her nosiness, but found that she had locked herself inside her cottage and when they peered through the window she was dancing round and so were all her tables and chairs! They were so unnerved that they left her in peace. Jonas Reeves, a diviner of Steeple Barton, was able to make a stool walk round the table.

A witch at Stoke Lyne was also seen floating in the air on a dough kip by a farmer, who was forced to swear not to tell anyone lest she bewitch him, and only revealed the secret on his death-bed. Mother Buckland, a beggar from Tetsworth, who was reputed to be a witch saw Phoebe Hawes pegging a shawl on her washing line and requested it. When refused she warned: 'Look out, you'll know. Look out!' Phoebe behaved like one lost for weeks until Mother Buckland came round again and was given the shawl, after which she recovered.

Sarey Bowers of Kirtlington lived at Fox Town's End where the hunt met, and a fox was often started there, but never caught so Sarey was accused both of bewitching foxes and hounds and being able to shape-change into a fox. A wounded fox once ran into her house, but when the huntsmen threw open the door there was nothing to be seen but Sarey sitting quietly by her fire with a sore leg. She terrorised local people who suffered if they displeased her.

Shaking Charlotte of North Leigh was an old gypsy woman with palsy who was a reputed witch in the mid-nineteenth century. It was said that if she was pricked her spells would be rendered harmless. A man, probably her husband, died and a half-burned book of spells was found on his funeral pyre.

A witch at Milton-under-Wychwood once 'stopped' a carter's horse so that it refused to go through a gate. The carter was so furious he hit her with his fork, killing her, but went unpunished because she was known as a witch.

Mother Galloway of Cuddesdon took against a local farmer, whose butter would not 'come' although he churned all day, until a friend suggested he put some pins in the churn, and when he did the butter 'came' straight away, and Mother Galloway was found covered with scratches.

George James Dew of Lower Heyford had a common sense view of life, and his diary (published as *Oxfordshire Village Life*) reveals that witchcraft was blamed for mental illnesses:

> April 8th 1876. The belief in witchcraft in this enlightened age, has not yet become extinct at Souldern. A poor, uneducated and somewhat delicate girl, named Mary Ellen Rouse, about 17 years of age, being unwell and her mind, perhaps, perverted, some of the people believe she has been bewitched. Samuel Rouse her father thinks he knows who has bewitched her. I could not persuade him to tell me who he thought it was, nor yet to disbelieve in witchcraft. He appears to have a firm belief in the supernatural. The girl's mind is somewhat deranged, but not sufficiently so, the Medical Officer says, to demand removal.

In the late nineteenth century a woman living in Spelsbury almshouses made wax images of people she disliked and stuck pins in them. An image found in 1954, in a tree at Coombe on land belonging to the Duke of Marlborough, resembled a female form, neatly bound with horsehair, with a straw or paper skirt and a hat or bonnet, but no-one could shed any light about its origins.

There were ways of protecting oneself against witchcraft: Tom Horley of Garsington thought that witches were hag-riding his horses at night because they were covered with sweat in the mornings, so he hung up a horse's heart in the stables and stabbed it (probably with thorns). After that his horses were untroubled. At North Leigh people told children to break up shells of boiled eggs so that they could not be used as boats by witches.

George James Dew wrote that Ann Tuslin of Lower Heyford, who died in 1875, was terrified of witches, and tried to protect herself and her family by sticking pins in a sheep's liver and putting crossed knives at every crack to prevent witches entering. John Kibble described witch balls, made of coloured glass and filled with water, which hung from the rafters to protect against witchcraft, and were considered more effective than horseshoes.

The Devil

The Devil has been associated with prehistoric sites such as the Devil's Punchbowl, a large hollow in the Downs above Letcombe Basset, while a large stone near Chinnor Hill is said to have been thrown by him at Chinnor Church but missed its target. The Devil rattled the chains at the gallows which stood in Rackham's Lane near St Margaret's church in Oxford. In the Middle Ages there was real fear of the Devil and at Adderbury church protection is provided by a pentalpha on the cornice.

The Devil is said to have moved churches at Ambrosden, Benson, Blackthorn, Checkendon and Ipsden. The story is similar in each case: at Blackthorn (where a church was never actually built) the church was intended to be built in a field now known as Church Leys, materials were taken there and foundations laid, but the Devil moved them overnight, and each time they were hauled back to the original site the Devil moved them again, so eventually the men gave in. At Checkendon the church should have been built, apparently, on a site known as the Devil's Churchyard (an Iron Age enclosure), but local inhabitants wanted it in a more accessible location, and again the Devil was said to have moved the materials every night. Ipsden Street is said to have had a thriving settlement which

In medieval times there was a strong belief in the Devil. The churches of Adderbury, Bloxham (illustrated) and Kings Sutton (in Northamptonshire) were considered so beautiful that they could not have been built by human hand alone. It is said that one day the finest workman tripped and the contents of his wheelbarrow were magically transformed into Crouch Hill near Banbury and the workman disappeared leaving a whiff of sulphur behind.

Crouch Hill, supposedly created by the Devil while he was building Bloxham church, from Alfred Beesley's History of Banbury (1841).

declined and when the residents tried to repair the dilapidated church the Devil undid all their labours and eventually moved the entire structure to the hill above, where it still stands. The stories may originate in the fact that churches were sometimes built on the site of pagan sites of worship and at Ipsden stones from an earlier church may have been incorporated into the current church.

There is a curious story from Adderbury which is more likely to have been a case of spontaneous combustion. According to a seventeenth-century pamphlet a woman who kept an alehouse cheated a customer of threepence change, but when challenged swore her innocence, adding 'May the Devil burn me if it be not so!' She threw out the customer and locked the front door. When her husband arrived home he had to force his way in and to his horror discovered: 'the Reliques of his wife, one side of her body and the Cloaths thereupon, from the Soal of her Foot to the Crown of her head being consumed and burnt to ashes, and nothing left but the Skeleton; whereas the other side remained whole, though it was observed that the flesh and skin was turned black, as if it had been blasted with lightning.' It was assumed that the Devil had claimed his due.

John Scarve or Scoure of North Hinksey is said to have sold his soul to the Devil for wealth, on condition that he provided for the local wisewomen and witches. John drew an enchanted circle within which he dared to defy the Devil and prevented the witches from communicating with him. However, when he stepped outside his circle the Devil pounced on him, trying to drag him up the chimney, but it was too small to take him and twisted round and round as the Devil pulled, and so it remained until the house was demolished. Scarve was pulled apart, the Devil flew off with his soul, and the witches were released. His body was buried beneath the wall of the church, neither inside nor outside and his ghost searched for his soul around Hinksey Manor.

North Leigh abounds with stories of the Devil, familiarly known as 'Old Nick' or 'Old Scrat'. Villagers believed that he could be summoned by reciting the Lord's Prayer backwards, or if a girl spent a long time looking in her mirror she would see the Devil reflected behind her. Children believed that if they ran twelve times round a certain tomb in North Leigh churchyard then looked through a hole in the wall they would see the Devil. He appeared as a fiery serpent to a man travelling from North Leigh to Barnard Gate, surrounding him so that he was transfixed for a while.

Sunday observance was reinforced by threats of what might happen in North Leigh if it was ignored: if people went nutting on a Sunday the Devil would pull down the branches so that they could be reached easily; men who caught a badger on a Sunday put it in a sack and were astonished when it vanished mysteriously leaving a whiff of sulphur behind. Local boys playing cricket on a Sunday were joined by a stranger who proved a very fine player but vanished in a puff of smoke.

Near New Yatt is a place called Devil's Corner, and those out on evil business at midnight may meet the Devil there in the shape of a black dog. The way to protect yourself against him was to spit three times and cross your fingers.

Sunday observance was behind Sid Hedges' story of Brooks the Bicester shoe-maker who was walking one Sunday to Merton via Gravenhill when he met a stranger who asked his business. When he replied that he was off to measure a man for boots the stranger asked him to measure his feet, and Brooks stopped to do it, but was horrified to be confronted with a cloven hoof!

Ghosts

Despite scientific experimentation, ghostly manifestations are difficult to record precisely. One theory is that dramatic situations and deaths, which involve an outpouring of energy, somehow become imprinted on the surrounding area, particularly the stones of buildings. A feature of ghost stories recorded over many years is that they seem to fade, as a recording might deteriorate: there are many stories of ghosts of white or grey ladies where the story has disappeared and the ghosts themselves seem to be fading.

Perhaps this explains the paucity of ancient ghosts, although at least one Roman soldier ghost, and possibly a chariot of Roman soldiers has been seen at North Leigh, which has a Roman villa nearby. Another ancient ghost is that of an Anglo-Saxon girl at Eynsham. During excavations the body of a girl with a spiked chain was discovered, buried alone, perhaps suggesting that she had committed some crime. Her skeleton was stored in a caravan on the site, where one of the diggers slept. During the night the caravan was shaken with great force, but there was nothing outside, and deep unexplained scratch marks were found on its roof. When gravel digging commenced on the site some workers were frightened by a white misty figure visible at dusk, and they disliked the cold sinister atmosphere at the location.

The story of the wild huntsmen from Noke has resonances with legends of the Norse god Woden, who led his horsemen through the skies as an omen of death and disaster. Benedict Winchcombe, who lived in the Manor House, died in 1623 and was buried in the church. He was said to be so addicted to hunting that he hunted seven days a week and continued careering round with his hounds after his death, until his ghost was laid by twelve parsons. Otmoor was formerly a wetland, and the nocturnal flight of geese, which abounded there, was once known as 'Gabriel hounds', and the two may be interconnected.

However, the Wild Hunt may have changed over the years into the 'spectral coach' which has been seen in many guises throughout the county. The Adderbury coach-and-four is that of Sir George Cobb of Cobb Hall, who accidentally drowned in 1762, but appeared when changes were made to his property of which he disapproved. He appeared, with his horses breathing fire, to terrified poachers, who became reformed characters. At Baynards Green it is said to be an eighteenth-century coach, where the coachman was shot in the head and killed when the coach was held up by highwaymen. The Dorchester coach is drawn by two grey horses. Spectral coaches have also been seen at Drayton St Leonard, Finstock, Horley and Leafield (where it was crowded with people and the sounds of the horn blowing and the harness rattling were heard). At Spelsbury the Chadlington baker once drove straight through a phantom coach-and-four, which was said to have overturned and been buried in a bog, but other versions mention a horse-drawn wagon. The Ramsden chariot, its horses emitting fire from their mouths, appeared at midnight and the occupant shouted 'Throw it out, throw it out' to the occupant of a particular house, who responded: 'I shan't, thee hadst it for thy time and I'll have it for mine.' The Napier coach seen between Oxford and Sandford-on-Thames contained the headless body of Sir George Napier who was hanged, drawn and quartered in 1610 for being a Catholic priest. His relatives secretly rescued his remains, apart from his head, for burial in the chapel attached to the farm. It is considered a death omen to see the coach, and if it is heard the person should avert his eyes or lie face down on the ground until it has passed. The Wilcote coach haunted to right a wrong: inside was Lord Wilcote, who it is said left land for the poor, but when his wishes were not respected his soul could not rest. His horses breathed fire and he cried 'Cast up, cast up!' Clergymen asked his lordship how they could lay him to rest and he is alleged to have told them to destroy the bell in Wilcote church, which was duly recast and the clapper was thrown into the pond. The coach of Woodcote House, drawn by four grey horses, stops in the avenue and after six ghostly occupants have alighted the coach proceeds, dragging chains behind.

Perhaps the most notorious ghostly chariot is that of Lord and Lady Tanfield, which haunted Burford and Great Tew. Lord Tanfield's illustrious career is described on his magnificent tomb in Burford church, translated as:

> In war and peace he was foremost among Englishmen, the pride of the Law and of the Courts, famed as a wise lawyer and a just statesman. He was no venal judge who would yield to a scoundrel's bribe… Under him no malefactor profited by corruption and no court made illicit gain; his wealth was honestly acquired and his honour was untarnished. He alone among rich men remained guiltless. He was equally worthy in his private life, conscientious and strict, but just, attentively overseeing his estates…

He and his wife Elizabeth rebuilt Burford Priory as a private house and lived there from 1585, entertaining James I in 1603. Local residents would not have agreed with the inscription his tomb as he rapaciously wrested control of Burford from

Lord and Lady Tanfield haunted Burford in a fiery chariot. Their tomb effigy in Burford church shows Lord Tanfield in the robes of a High Court judge. He was knighted, served as Member of Parliament for New Woodstock and later for Oxfordshire and as Chief Baron of the Exchequer from 1607.

The ghosts of Lord and Lady Tanfield were enticed into a bottle which was thrown into the river by Burford Bridge. One dry season the water began to bubble and residents were so frightened that the bottle would surface, releasing the Tanfields' spirits, that they topped up the river with water.

the Corporation and the oppressed residents of Great Tew petitioned against him in 1624. On his death in 1625 they must have heaved a sigh of relief, but it was short-lived, as he and his wife drove a fiery coach through the air up and down the street above Burford, terrifying the inhabitants and creating such a nuisance that seven clergymen, using bell, book and candle, persuaded the spirits of the Tanfields into a glass bottle which was dropped under the first arch of Burford Bridge.

Many ghosts are associated with monastic sites, such as a nun at Ambrosden who is said to have committed suicide, a Bruern monk who walked along the route of an underground passage between the abbey and Tangley Hall, monks at Bicester and Burford, nuns at Checkendon, a monk who walks in Dorchester Abbey and so on, seldom with any story to accompany them.

An Elizabethan lady was seen in the mid-twentieth century in a house in South Bar in Banbury. Nannies seldom stayed long, complaining that they had felt someone sit on their beds. The daughter of the house went downstairs to the lavatory one night, and when she came out saw a woman in Elizabethan dress standing on the stairs, barring her way. She went back into the bathroom and closed the door, peering out several times, seeing the ghost in her way each time. Soon she felt cold and plucked up her courage to go back upstairs, walking right through the apparition, which felt damp and clingy like a cobweb.

Jane Culpeper, who died in 1636 and is commemorated by a marble tomb in Church Hanborough, was reputed to be a witch. She disliked children and forbade them to shout, or to skate on the frozen duck-pond. Her ghost, nick-named 'Up Joan' and 'Old Mother Scallpepper', dressed in black with a poke bonnet, walked on the top of hedges along the footpath from Church Hanborough to Eynsham and was laid in a pond, but when the pond dried she haunted again, making strange noises. She was last seen by an evacuee boy during the Second World War.

A ghost said to haunt a Wigginton house in the twentieth century was that of a woman whose daughter had drowned in the well. She was there to protect other children, and was felt as a friendly presence. Her ghost disappeared when repairs were done to the roof.

The ghost of Worsham Lane, Asthall, has several possible identities. Some say he is a shepherd who was skinned alive by a gang of sheep-stealers because he warned Bruern Abbey about their projected theft, or it may be the ghost of highwayman Black Stocking, a Swinbrook gentleman who occasionally robbed highways in his fine clothes and a black mask.

Many ghosts are associated with the Civil War such as a cavalier at Chipping Norton. The ghost of John Hampden, who was mortally wounded at the Battle of Chalgrove, appears at Clifton Hampden. A troop of phantom roundhead soldiers marched through an East Hendred house, minus their feet - apparently the floor level had been raised since the seventeenth century. In Bicester a ghost associated with Rookery Pond may be that of the lady of Bicester House who hid her jewels and valuables in the pond. The Roundheads who attacked the house were so furious at finding nothing to plunder, and at her refusal to tell them the whereabouts of her treasure, that they murdered her so the White Lady rides sadly round the pond. At Towersey near Thame a young soldier fled from his enemies (it is not recorded whether he was Cavalier or Roundhead) and hid in a

William de la Pole, Duke of Suffolk, and his wife Alice founded a school and almshouses at Ewelme, finished in 1442. William became a scapegoat as England fared badly in war with France and, despite Henry VI trying to save him by banishment, he was captured and beheaded as he fled to Flanders. His headless ghost has appeared in the cloisters.

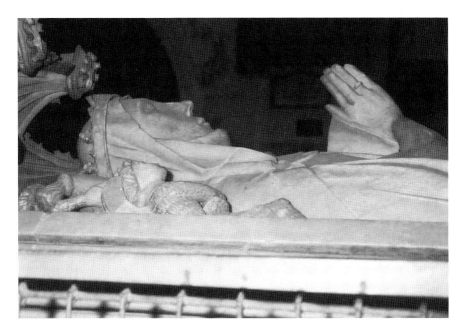

Alice de la Pole, a Knight of the Garter in her own right, descended from Geoffrey Chaucer, has appeared as the ghost of a tall veiled woman dressed in black.

The chapel, consecrated in 1449, and remaining wing of the great house at Rycote boast several ghosts, including that of a monk (perhaps from the Benedictine monastery there), Sir Robert Dudley and Sir Thomas More (executed for his opposition to Henry VIII) who visited his daughter Cecily Heron here. Cecily may be the grey lady in Elizabethan dress, nicknamed Arabella, who glides through the chapel.

barn, but the neighing of his horse gave him away and he was shot and buried in the churchyard.

Prudence, a Puritan housemaid died of a broken heart when deserted by her cavalier lover and her presence can be felt in a house in Magpie Lane, Oxford, where she has been sighted in plain brown dress. She may have been Prudence Burcote whose death is recorded in the Parish Register of 1643.

The notorious Mary Blandy, daughter of solicitor Francis Blandy, Town Clerk of Henley-on-Thames, fell in love with the wastrel Captain William Cranstoun, He was already married to a Roman Catholic, but persuaded Mary that he could annul the marriage and gave her a cairngorm brooch as a love token. Francis Blandy had severe doubts about his suitability, believing he was after Mary's money, so forbade Mary to have anything more to do with him. The lovers were not prepared to part and Cranstoun sent Mary a white powder, ostensibly to clean her brooch, but added that it was a love philtre which she could administer to her father to make him more amenable. The powder was arsenic, and Blandy died on 14 August 1751. The doctor was suspicious abut Blandy's death and Mary was confined to her room. She escaped, but the next February she was brought to trial where, despite her protestations of innocence, she was condemned, hanged at Oxford Prison on 6 April 1752 and buried in Henley. Cranstoun escaped and fled to the continent where he died of what may also have been arsenic poisoning.

Hanwell Castle is said to be haunted by a monk and a seventeenth-century lady who went mad after the deaths of her children.

Mary's distraught ghost haunts the White Hart in Henley, and she has been seen standing thoughtfully at the bottom of the garden of her house in Hart Street. When a play written about her story was performed in Henley an unexplained figure, perhaps that of Mary, was in the audience.

Sarah Fletcher, a beautiful and charming woman, was driven to suicide at the age of twenty-nine in 1799 by the cruelty and unfaithful behaviour of her husband, a naval captain, whose attempt to commit bigamy was frustrated by Sarah. She hanged herself with her pocket handkerchief which she attached to a curtain rod in her bedroom. The verdict at her inquest (by which time her uncaring husband was on his way to the West Indies) was lunacy, so she was buried in Dorchester Abbey. The inscription on her tomb reads: 'Contemplate this spot, in which are deposited the Remains of a Young Lady, whose artless Beauty, innocence of mind and gentle manner once obtained her the love and esteem of all who knew her; but when nerves were too delicately spun to bear the rude Shakes and Jostlings which we meet with in this transitory world, Nature gave way. She sunk and died a Martyr to Excessive Sensibility… May her soul meet that peace in Heaven which this earth denied her.' Sarah had lived at 'Courtiers' in Clifton Hampden, and her ghost was seen by Revd Edward Crake (who died in 1915), who lived there when it was a school run by his father. Footsteps of a woman in high-heeled shoes were heard in what had been her room, and waves of cold air

Lady Alice Harcourt is said to have been murdered in the fifteenth century in what is now known as Pope's Tower, Stanton Harcourt, by her chaplain, who cut up her body and threw it out of the window. She haunted the murder scene until her spirit was laid to rest in Lady Alice's Pool, one of the fishponds.

were felt. Sometimes the figure of a woman with reddish purple ribbon in her curly auburn hair wearing a long black silk cloak was visible. After Crake was ordained he tried to exorcise the ghost but the manifestations increased.

The unfortunate Hampden Pye of Faringdon fell victim to the greed of his stepmother, who wanted to inherit her husband's fortune, so she bribed his naval captain to ensure that he was in the line of fire in battle and his head was blown off. His ghost haunted both her and the captain, appearing with his head under his arm running before them as they returned home at night and sometimes clean plates were suddenly smeared with blood. Eventually the ghost was laid by twelve clergymen in a local pond. An alternative version is that he secretly married a servant girl to the outrage of his family and was sent to sea where his head was blown off by a cannonball during a battle with the Spanish fleet.

Augustus Hare reported that fresh blood was often seen on the staircase at Fritwell Manor and at other times the figure of an old man in a grey dressing gown with an open wound in his throat appeared. Apparently Sir Baldwin Wake, who had lived there, fell out with his brother over a lady they both loved, and, declaring that his brother was insane, imprisoned him in chains at the top of the house.

A more welcome ghost was seen at Beckley: one evening several of the family confronted a ghost which had often been seen in their cottage and asked it why it was troubled. The figure beckoned to them and passed outside through the closed door, so they followed it up the garden, where it pointed to the ground. They dug that spot and discovered a box full of money. A similar story refers to the Priory at Great Milton.

Poltergeist activity centred round the family of blacksmith Thomas Hall and his wife Ann who lived at Little Tew before 1894. At mealtimes loud cock-crow was often heard and it sounded as though dishes were being smashed. The Halls moved to Hook Norton, but the same noises were heard there. Mrs Hall's mother, Mrs Beach, heard groaning from under her pillow and when she struck a penknife into it blood appeared. Sometimes a hidden force seemed to stop the blacksmiths from hammering correctly and once fire-irons moved across the room.

There was also poltergeist activity at Beth-oni in Tackley, a three-hundred year old house. Strange voices were heard, doors slammed, there was a noise like an explosion, and the sounds of chains dragging, footsteps, knockings, boots were thrown about, heavy weights dropped and so on. Candles were suddenly extinguished, there were flashes of light and sometimes spectral figures appeared of a burly farmer and a contemptuous man in a cloak; a visitor felt something claw at her bedspread and some felt electric shocks. The house was exorcised in 1907 but manifestations returned, so another exorcism was performed, ending the manifestations.

The hospital at Chipping Norton, which was used for convalescent soldiers, is haunted by the ghost of a First World War soldier in khaki, mainly seen by those on their death-beds.

During the 1950s a signal box at Yarnton was haunted by sounds of heavy footsteps climbing the stairs, the door handle moved and the door shook. When the signalman investigated there was nothing to see, but he smelt pipe-tobacco.

Two stories echo the urban myth of the phantom hitch-hiker. Two sisters driving in West Hendred one night both saw a man in an overcoat and cap dash across the road right in front of their car, but there was no collision, although if it had been a real man they could not have avoided him. A girl driving through Clifton Hampden crossed the bridge and felt someone climb into her car and suddenly felt icy from the waist downwards. The figure, which looked like a vicar, climbed out at Marsh Bridge, Didcot. She later discovered that a local girl, who was said to have become pregnant by the local vicar, had committed suicide by throwing herself over the bridge.

Ghosts are not always human: a headless calf haunts North Leigh and black dogs have been seen at North Leigh, Wilcote and Leafield. The Wilcote dog was laid by clergymen reading prayers over a newborn child and throwing a clapper into each of two ponds. If the clappers are ever reunited it is said the ghost dog will return. A black dog seen in Barton Lane in Headington in the nineteenth century was said to have great saucer eyes.

It is interesting to note how new ghost stories have built up over they years, as old memories have faded.

twelve

LOCAL RHYMES

There are several types of local rhymes. Some are simple couplets such as:

> Oxford for learning, London for wit,
> Hull for women and York for a tit.

or:

> Shrivenham Revels and Bourton Rout,
> The Watchfield pot boils, and the fire is out.

or:

> Great Tew, Little Tew, Enstone and Barford,
> If you want a pretty girl you must go to Burford.

and:

> Sutton for mutton, Stanton Harcourt for beef,
> Standlake for a pretty girl and Northmoor for a thief.

Another refers to medieval landowners:

> The Tracys, the Lacys and the Fettiplaces,
> Own all the manors, the parks and the chases.

Some rhymes suggested rivalries between villages such as:

> Beckley Bucks are very fine bucks,
> Elsfield bucks are better;
> But if we catch the Marston bucks,
> We'll push them in the gutter.

or:

> Fulbrook suggs
> Born in tubs,
> Couldn't get out
> For lice and bugs.

(Another version refers to 'Steeple Bumpkins' from Steeple Aston)

and:

> Bloxham dogs,
> Come to Adderbury to buy your togs.

This rhyme was recorded by Hearne in 1717:

> Henley-on-Thames and Ackington Way,
> Are never without thief night or day.

It would be interesting to know the origin of:

> This is Stoke,
> Where they cut the smoke
> With wooden hatchets.

Some rhymes are doggerel, such as:

> There was a man of Taston,
> Neither fat not lean,
> And when he got to Spelsbury,
> He was half a mile from Dean.

Some rhymes refer to events in village history such as the Charlbury team beating the others at cricket:

> Brightwell and Sotwell and Merry Mackey,
> Poor lousy Charlbury whacked all three.

Mollie Harris, in *The Green Years* mentioned one about a Ducklington event:

> The floods were out at Ducklington
> One cold November day.
> And all the ducks in Ducklington
> Were lost or gone astray.

Some rhymes mention particular buildings such as churches:

> If Kidlington spire were twenty times higher,
> I'd take off my shoe and jump over it.

A rhyme was invented after the Ordnance Survey erected a white tent on top of Stonesfield tower to use as an observation post:

> Stonesfield tower wears a hat,
> Charlbury's tower's no better than that,
> Field-Town's steeple's ready to fall,
> But Ramsden steeple beats 'em all.

The church at East Hendred has a clock with bells which play hymn tunes every three hours; in the early twentieth century, according to R.E. Moreau, the children used to sing this rhyme to the tunes:

> The leaves are green,
> The nuts are brown,
> They are so high
> They won't come down.
> Leave them alone
> Till frosty weather,
> And they'll all come down together.

Pub rhymes were also popular. This one mentions all the public houses in Hook Norton, which still has its own brewery:

Banbury church tower, drawn by John Bloxham. The church was rebuilt in the eighteenth century, but it was ten years before the tower was added, leading to the rhyme:
Dirty Banbury's proud people
Built a church without a steeple.

The *Sun* comes out before the time [it is
   opposite the church clock]
The *Lion* comes out with a roar,
The *Bell* sings out with ting, ting, ling,
The *Pear Tree* hangs over the door.
The *Blackbird* sings its merry song,
To The *Wheatsheaf* he doth fly.
The *Railway Tavern* stands on a hill.
And The *Gate* it doth hang high.'

John Kibble mentioned an Enstone pub rhyme:

The *Harrow* to harrow,
The *Plough* to plow,
The *Swan* to swim,
The *Bell* to ring,
The *Litchfield Arms*,
And the *Talbot Inn*.

Another lists public houses owned by the Sparks family who brewed at East End:

Hit or Miss and the Golden Ball,
The Leather Bottle and Shepherd's All.

Some rhymes were invented to advertise towns such as this Bicester one mentioned by Sid Hedges:

Meat by the Mile,
Beer by the Pound,
When 'osses be okhard
Turn 'em around.

Meat was sold in the Shambles and beer from the Fox Inn and horses being broken in were made to circle the Hallelujah tree.
   The White Horse was used to advertise Goodman's Sauce:

Dear is the vendor's native town
(Though cheap the product of his skill)
There Alfred battled for his Crown
And graved the White Horse on our Hill –
Our Hill of picnic spots the chief,
Where fair ones couched on flowery moss
Enjoy our matchless Vale-fed beef,
Married to Goodman's matchless Sauce.

There are many miscellaneous village rhymes. Sometimes a rhyme has several variants such as the Wychwood rhyme:

> Hailey, Crawley, Curbridge and Cogges,
> Witney spinners and Ducklington dogs,
> Finstock on the hill, Fawler downderry,
> Beggarly Ramsden and Lousy Charlbury,
> Woodstock for bacon, Bladon for beef.
> Hanborough for a scurvy knave,
> And Combe for a thief.

A variation used to taunt other villagers went:

> Hailey and Crawley,
> Curbridge and Cogs
> Witney spinners
> And Duckelton dogs,
> Finstock for apples,
> Fawler for Corn,
> Lovely Stonesfield
> And lousy Ramshorn.
> Finstock upon the hill
> Fawler down derry
> Beggarly Stonesfield amd Lousy Charlbury.

There is a hint of resignation in:

> Aston, Yelford, Chimney and Shifford,
> Here we live and here we die, Lord,
> For life is but a single thread
> Which soon is snapped and we are dead.

There is insult in:

> Aynho on the hill,
> Souldern in the hole,
> And Fritwell wenches
> As black as coal.

A variation runs:

> Aynho on the hill,
> Clifton in the clay,
> Drunken Deddington,
> And Hempton highway.

Referring to a legend that the people of Deddington sold their church bells to pay for drink. Some songs were sung in schools, such as this one from Middleton Stoney:

> Mr — is a very good man, he tries to teach us all he can,
> Reading, writing, arithmetic, he don't forget
>   to give us the stick,
> When he hits us he makes us dance, out of
>   England into France,
> Out of France, into Spain, over the hills and back again.

Another one from Shipton-under-Wychwood ran:

> Multiplication is vexation, division's twice as bad,
> The rule of three, it puzzles me, and fractions drive me mad.

Banbury is in a class of its own when it comes to rhymes, partly because they were proliferated by the printing firms Rushers which specialised in chap-books in the late eighteenth and nineteenth centuries giving rhymes a local slant. Primarily, though, it is renowned for rhymes about Banbury cross. The earliest version, published in 1784 in Joseph Ritson's *Gammer Gurton's Garland* reads:

> Ride a cock horse to Banbury Cross,
> To see an old woman get up on her horse,
> Rings on her fingers and bells on her toes,
> And so she makes music wherever she goes.

The 'fine lady' makes her first appearance in 1797 in the Revd Baptist Noel Turner's *Infant Institutes, Part the First, or a Nurserical Essay on the Poetry, Lyric and Allegorical, or the Earlier Ages*:

> Hight a cock horse to Banbury Cross,
> To see a fine lady upon a white horse,
> Rings on her fingers and bells on her toes,
> She will have music wherever she goes.

The Tom Tit's Song Book, published around 1800, included:

> Ride a cock horse
> To Banbury Cross,
> To see an old woman
> Get up on her horse,
> A ring on her finger,
> A bonnet of straw,
> The strangest old woman
> That ever you saw.

Yet another version describes a Fiennes lady:

> Ride a cock horse to Banbury Cross,
> To see a Fiennes lady on a white horse,

> With rings on her fingers and bells on her toes,
> She shall have music wherever she goes.

The Fiennes family have owned Broughton Castle near Banbury since the fifteenth century, and in the seventeenth century Celia, daughter of Nathaniel
Fiennes, made a name for herself riding round the country with her servant,
writing about all the places she visited, so she may be the lady referred to here. A
French version was published in *Country Life*:

> Allons à dada à Bains-brie à la croix,
> Voir une vielle à cheval des bagues à ses doights,
> Et des sonettes aux orteils à fin qu'elle fasse,
> La musique sans cesse partout ou elle passe.

A version was even heard on BBC Radio Four adapted as a complaint about traf-
fic reorganisation:

> Ride a cock horse to Banbury Cross,
> To see a fine lady on a white horse.
> With rings on her fingers and bells on her feet,
> Who can't find her way in a one-way street.

Various attempts have been made to explain the rhyme, some suggesting that it
contains memories of a spring festival, perhaps on May Day, with the lady riding
round the fields, reinforced by a fifteenth-century illustration from the Musée
Condé, Chantilly which shows a lady on a white horse in a procession. Bells
in this context might have been symbols of rank, and are found on the taper-
ing shoes of the fifteenth century, or were perhaps to frighten away evil spirits.
Although Banbury people were proud of their maypole and there was a great fuss
when the Puritans tried to demolish it, no other evidence supports this theory,
and the rhyme was published so long afterwards that it must remain dubious.

Banbury had several crosses, the principal one in Cornhill, (the upper area of
the Market Place), the Bread Cross which was a market cross with a slate roof in
Butcher's Row, and the White Cross which formed a boundary mark in West Bar.
They were probably all destroyed by the Puritans, as the main cross was in 1600.
The current cross was erected to celebrate the marriage of Queen Victoria's eld-
est daughter, Princess Victoria, the Princess Royal, to Frederick William, Prince of
Prussia in 1858, so the rhymes preserve the memory of an earlier Banbury cross.
The cock horse was the term sometimes used for an additional horse kept at the
bottom of a steep hill to help haul coaches up it, or it could mean one person riding
behind another. Other rhymes promoted Banbury's famous markets and fairs:

> To market, to market,
> To buy a fat pig;
> Home again, home again,
> Jiggety jig.
> To Banbury market,
> To buy a fat hog,

The fine lady on a white horse shown on a
printing plate in Banbury Museum depicting the
famous rhyme:
Ride a cock horse to Banbury Cross,
To see a fine lady ride on a white horse,
Rings on her fingers, bells on her toes;
She shall have music wherever she goes.

Home again, home again,
Jiggety jog.

and:

As I was going to Banbury,
Upon a summer's day,
My dame had butter, eggs and fruit
And I had corn and hay,
Joe drove the ox and Tom the swine,
Dick took the foal and mare.
I sold them all – then home to dine
From famous Banbury Fair.

Banbury was also famous for its horse fair:

Ride a cock horse to Banbury Cross,
To buy little Johnny a galloping horse,
It trots behind and it ambles before,
And Johnny shall ride until he can ride no more.

and:

Hight o-cock horse, to Banbury Cross,
To buy a new nag, and nimble horse.

Banbury's notorious enthusiasm for Puritanism in the sixteenth and
seventeenth centuries was parodied in the following rhyme:

To Banbury came I, o prophane one!
Where I saw a Puritane one
Hanging of his cat on Monday
For killing of a mouse on Sunday.

Banbury is also renowned for its cakes:

> Ride a cock horse to Banbury Cross
> To see what Emma can buy,
> A penny white cake I'll buy for her sake,
> And a two-penny tart or pie.

And this one published by John Golby Rusher:

> Now make a nice bun, my baker's man,
> A Banbury Cake, fast as you can;
> Currants and sugar, mark it with T,
> Then bring it home, To Tommy and me.

Banbury's medieval bridge is mentioned in the rhyme:
Sing see-saw Jack thatching the ridge,
Which is the way to Banbury bridge?
One foot up and t'other foot down,
And that's the way to Banbury town.
The illustration is from A. Beesley's *The History of Banbury* (1841)

The opening of Banbury Co-operative and Industrial Society in the mid-nineteenth century was celebrated in rhyme:

> Ride a cock horse to Banbury cross
> To see the Co-op and its very fine horse,
> With hundreds of members and friends round about
> It ever will prosper without any doubt.

There is even a butter-making rhyme about Banbury:

> Come butter churn,
> Come butter churn,
> The great Bull of Banbury
> Shan't have none.

Folk Song

Before the advent of cinema, radio and television, people provided their own entertainment, and many enjoyed singing. Flora Thompson described how the villagers of Juniper Hill in the late nineteenth century spent most evenings in their local pub, drinking the half pint of beer which was all they could afford, talking politics and singing folk songs. Each man had his own special song, some of which she recorded, although without the tunes. One song was about Lord Lovell, possibly popular because of the connection with Minster Lovell:

> Lord Lovell stood at his castle gate,
> Calming his milk-white steed,
> When up came Lady Nancy Bell,
> To wish her lover God-speed.

> 'And where are you going, Lord Lovell?' she said.
> 'And where are you going?' said she.
> 'Oh, I'm going away from my Nancy Bell,
> Away to a far country-tre-tre;
> Away to a far coun-tre.'

> 'And when will you come back, Lord Lovell?' she said,
> 'When will you come back?' said she.
> 'Oh, I will come back in a year and a day,
> Back to my Lady Nancy-ce-ce-ce.
> Back to my Lady Nan-cee.'

Lord Lovell was away much longer than he had anticipated, and returned to hear the church bells tolling for a death:

> 'And who is it dead?' Lord Lovell, he said.
> 'And who is it dead,' said he.
> And some said 'Lady Nancy Bell,'
> And some said 'Lady Nan-cee.'

> Lady Nancy died as it were to-day;
> And Lord Lovell he died to-morrow,
> And she, she died for pure, pure grief,
> And he, he died for sorrow.

> And they buried her in the chancel high,
> And they buried him in the choir;
> And out of her grave sprung a red, red rose,
> And out of his sprung a briar.

> And they grew till they grew to the church roof,
> And then they couldn't grow any higher;

So they twined themselves in a true lovers' knot,
For all lovers true to admire.

Songs were sung after local sporting occasions, in the home, and at seasonal festivities such as Whit Ales and harvest homes and waits went round singing at
Christmas. Janet Blount collected folk songs in Adderbury, and Alfred Williams in
the Thames valley such as the Eynsham Poaching Song he learned from Henry
Leach of Eynsham:

> Three Eynsham chaps went out one day,
> To Lord Abingdon's manor they made their way;
> They took some dogs to catch some game,
> And soon to Wytham Woods they came.
>
> We had not long been beating there,
> Before our spaniel put up a hare;
> Up she jumped, and away she ran,
> At the very same time a pheasant sprang.
>
> We had not beat the woods all through,
> Before Barrett, the keeper, came in view;
> When we saw the old beggar look,
> We made our way to Cassington Brook.
>
> When we got there 'twas full to the brim,
> And you'd have laughed to see us swim:
> Ten feet of water, if not more;
> When we got out, our dogs came o'er.
>
> Over hedges, ditches, gates and rails,
> Our dogs followed after, behind our heels.
> If he had catched us, say what you will,
> He'd have sent us all to Abingdon Jail.

Village Tales

Some villages such as Combe, which has been nicknamed 'Silly Combe' or 'Coot
Combe' have attracted a variety of daft tales although 'silly' originally meant
blessed. Once people heard the village band playing in the hall and went in to tell
them how good they sounded, so the bandsmen rushed out so that they could
hear themselves! Villagers are also said to have lifted a pig onto a wall so that he
could watch the band go by. Another man covered a bucket of water he was carrying with his coat so that it would not get wet.

Shilton has also acquired the nickname 'Silly', because the villagers are said to
have driven fish under the bridge to stop them getting wet when it rained.

At North Leigh a man came to visit the windmill, which was stationary when
he arrived, so he tied the donkey to the mill's sail and went in. However the miller

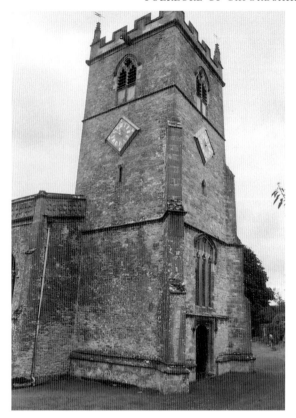

The villagers of Combe are
said to have thought that their
fourteenth-century church tower
was too squat, so they spread
manure around the base of it to
make it grow. During the night
the manure was washed away
in heavy rain and next morning
they exclaimed delightedly:
'Look, 'ee's growed!'

started up the mill and the donkey was lifted up into the air before the sails could
be stopped. A North Leigh girl visiting Oxford was asked where she came from
and on replying her questioner commented: 'Oh, that's where the donkey went
up on the windmill!' In the 1920s the bus conductor used to ask North Leigh
villagers if they wanted to get off to see the donkey.

There was a story that the people of Tackley had only one needle between
them in the entire village and that it got so hot with use that they had to cool it
in the brook.

Ducklington and Mollington both have the nickname 'moonraker', probably
reflecting an old tale that villagers looking into a pool saw the full moon reflected
in it and mistook it for a large cheese, so tried to fish it out.

thirteen

UNIVERSITY CUSTOMS

Oxford University is the oldest in England, although not dating back as far as the reign of King Alfred as forged deeds, written by University College in 1381, maintained to win a lawsuit. As late as 1872 University College celebrated its 'millennium' with elaborate toasts to King Alfred 'whose memory will dwell like honey in the mouths of both clerics and people.' After that the Alfredian myth gradually died and 1170 was accepted as the foundation date, when, following a dispute between Henry II and Louis VII of France, Henry demanded that English scholars at the University of Paris return home. Many settled in Oxford. Some medieval traditions lasted a long time: for six hundred years each graduate had to swear that he would never be reconciled with Henry, son of Simeon, who had committed murder in Oxford in 1242.

St Scholastica's Day Riot

The most notorious event was the major riot between Town and Gown on St Scholastica's Day, 10 February 1355, which had repercussions through the centuries. It began in the Swyndlestock Tavern in Carfax (commemorated by a plaque) when students and clerks including Walter de Springheuse and Roger de Chesterfield disparaged the quality of the wine provided by innkeeper John de Croydon, who responded indignantly with 'stubborn and saucy language', upon which wine was thrown over his head. Townsmen came to his rescue and the bell of St Martin's was rung to summon further aid and unarmed students were attacked with bows and arrows. The chancellor, who tried to calm proceedings, was forced to flee and students were summoned to help by the bell of St Mary the Virgin, and armed fighting continued all day.

The Mayor of Oxford rode next day to Woodstock to present the town's grievances to Edward III, who was in residence. Country people supported the townsmen and students' hostels were broken into, students were thrown into lavatories and dunghills, more than sixty scholars and some townsmen were killed and hundreds wounded and books and property in nineteen halls despoiled. Once peace was restored after three days the city was put under interdict, which entailed closing all the churches for a year, while an enquiry was held. Prominent citizens were imprisoned and hefty fines imposed: an immediate payment of 500

The St Scholastica's Day riot of 1355, (in the modern calendar) depicted for the Oxford Pageant of 1907.

marks followed by annual payments of 100 marks to compensate for damage. It resulted in the University gaining more power and taking over some municipal functions. The humiliation of the town continued: until 1825, on the anniversary of the riot the Mayor, Bailiffs and Burgesses walked in solemn procession from the Guildhall to St Mary's Church where they knelt to pray for each of the victims and each gave a silver penny, then the Mayor swore to uphold the privileges of the University.

The aggravation between Town and Gown has gone, although even in the nineteenth century there was discord, Mervyn Power, a Brasenose student was stabbed to death on Bonfire Night in 1857, after which students were 'gated' (refused permission to leave college) on 5 November to avoid more fights.

James Morris commented on privileges still held by the University in 1965 such as the ability to close the University Parks at will, but allowing resident members of Convocation to have keys so that they could enter at any time. The University had administrative roles over the Town such as electing Clerks of the Market, and during University terms licensing all stage performances within twenty miles of Oxford. Undergraduates could demand that their cases be heard by the Chancellors' Court if they had been arrested by the police or were sued in civil cases.

Encaenia

The principal formal event in the university year is Encaenia, held in June, when honorary degrees are presented, the modern version of the medieval Act where degrees were presented, accompanied by great festivities. It was moved from the

The Encaenia Procession, around 1906, showing the university personnel in full academic dress.

University church, St Mary the Virgin, to the Sheldonian Theatre in 1699. A procession begins at the Vice-Chancellor's College, and heads to the Sheldonian Theatre. The University Marshall leads the procession, followed by eight bedels carrying staves, then the Chancellor in a black and gold robe, the High Steward, the Vice-Chancellor, the University Burgesses, the Doctors of Divinity, Medicine, Civil Law, Letters, Science, Music and Philosophy, the Senior and Junior Proctors, the Heads of Houses (Colleges), Masters of Arts, Bachelors of Arts, Scholars, Commoners and the Registrar. The dignitaries receiving honorary degrees sign their names in a book in the Divinity School then process to the Sheldonian, where the Public Orator introduces them individually with a short Latin speech replete with puns, while the Chancellor makes a speech in response, shakes the person by the hand and motions him to a seat. The Public Orator recites the Creweian Oration, a review of the year in Latin, the University prize-winners read extracts from their essays, then after the ceremony luncheon parties are held. Today the ceremony is a solemn one, but in the past it has sometimes been somewhat rowdy.

Boy Bishops and Christmas Kings

Boy bishops were elected at New College, All Souls and Magdalen College before the Reformation, following a custom dating back to the tenth century in which choirboys chose one of their number to act as 'bishop' from 5 December, St Nicholas' Day, until 28 December, Holy Innocents' Day. He conducted ceremonies as though he were a bishop, and if he died in office would be buried as one.

Lords of Misrule, usually elected at Halloween and ruling until Candlemas, 2 February, masterminded revelries from New Year to Twelfth Night. At Christ Church, Magdalen, New College and St John's they were known as Christmas Kings, at Trinity as Christmas Princes and at Merton as Rex Fabarum.

Anthony Wood wrote in *History and Antiquities of the University of Oxford* that:

> The outgoing Rex despatched letters under a seal purporting to be sent from some place abroad, and his envoys appeared 'duly robed' and delivered them to the Bachelor Fellow. Those then, standing, sometimes walking, round the fire, there reading the contents of them, would choose the senior fellow that had not yet borne that office, whether he was a Doctor of Divinity, Law or Physick, and being so elected had power put into his hands of punishing all misdemeanours done in time of Christmas, either by imposing exercises on the juniors, or putting into the stocks at the end of the hall any of the servants, with other punishments that were sometimes very ridiculous. He always had a chair provided for him, and would sit in great state when any speeches were spoken or justice to be executed, and so this his authority would continue until Candlemas.

In 1607 a Christmas Prince, elected at St John's College for the first time in thirty years, took office on 30 November. His officers were proclaimed and given burlesque titles on 21 December, and the Prince's chamber was lavishly furnished complete with a chair of state, symbol of royalty. On Christmas Day he was chief guest at a feast, then over the following days several plays were performed, and he stood down from office on Shrove Tuesday, when his honours were buried and the Prince acted as his own chief mourner. The Prince, Thomas Tooker, was given many titles, parodying those of royalty, based on places in Oxford:

> The most magnificent and renowned Thomas, by the favour of Fortune, Prince of Alba Fortunata, Lord of St John's, High Regent of the Hall, Duke of St Giles's, Marquis of Magdalen, Landgrave of the Grove, Count Palatine of the Cloysters, Chief Bailiff of Beaumont, High Ruler of Rome (land north of Oxford), Master of the Manor of Walton, Governor of Gloucester Green, sole Commander of all Titles, Tournaments, and Triumphs, Superintendent of all solemnities whatsoever.

A King of the Beans was chosen at Merton (presumably on Twelfth Night) until 1557, the last being Jason Heywood.

Freshmen Rituals and Student Customs

Freshmen arriving at the University had to endure induction rituals such as holding out their chins so that a senior member could gouge off a piece of skin from the lip to the chin with his right thumb-nail, then make the student drink a beer glass of salt water. Such rites were discontinued in the seventeenth century during the Commonwealth. At Merton College freshmen were punished in that way if the speech they made in hall was dull.

Sconcing was the punishment for bad manners, often at the dining table, such as talking about politics, women or work: the offender was obliged to drink a large quantity of beer from an enormous container. If he managed to consume it all he would not have to pay for the beer. In the eighteenth century a scholar could be discommonsed, or denied the privilege of taking his allowance in the college hall for a few days; this was the punishment for a Trinity student who neglected to say grace after dinner while in waiting.

'Sporting the oak' is the term used when a student closes both the inner and outer door of his college room to indicate that he does not wish to be disturbed.

Glove presentation

The *Gentleman's Magazine* of 1761 recorded that the presidents of Corpus Christi, Magdalen and Trinity College, attended by their senior fellows, would wait on the Bishop of Winchester, their visitor and patron, and present him with the traditional gift of a pair of laced gloves.

All Souls

At Christmas everyone working at the college is presented with a mince pie on a plate bearing All Souls' coat of arms.

The most famous custom, Hunting the Mallard, is now only held once a century, (and should next happen on 14 January 2101), although it may once have been annual. The Mallard Song is sung each year on All Souls' Day and at the Bursar's Gaudy.

The origin of Fellows 'Hunting the Mallard' right through the college from cellars to roof, searching every nook and cranny, for several hours, accompanied by much drinking, is obscure, but legend says that a duck was discovered during the

The obverse and reverse of an electrotype of the pewter mallard medal issued in 1701, showing the Lord Mallard being chaired by Fellows and the mallard on a pole.

laying of the college drains in 1438. It is perhaps more plausibly connected with the discovery in the sixteenth or seventeenth century, while digging a college drain, of a thirteenth-century seal depicting a griffin and the name of 'Guil. Malardi'.

The first reference to Mallard Night is from 1616, when participants were accused of creating a disturbance and fined. The song sung during the hunt has varied over the years. This version was based by Martin West on six extant versions:

> The Griffine, Bustard, Turkey and Capon
> Lett other hungry Mortalls gape on
> And on theire bones with Stomacks fall hard,
> But lett Allsouls' Men have ye Mallard.
> Hough the bloud of King Edward, by ye bloud of King Edward
> It was a swapping, swapping mallard.
>
> Some storys strange are told I trow
> By Baker, Holinshead & Stow
> Of Cocks and Bulls and other queire things
> That happen'd in ye Reignes of theire Kings,
> Hough the bloud etc.
>
> The Romans once admir'd a gander
> More than they did theire best Commander,
> Because hee saved, if some don't foolle us,
> The place named from ye Scull of Tolus.
> Ho the bloud etc.
>
> The Poets fain'd Jove turn'd a Swan,
> But lett them prove it if they can.
> To mak't appeare it's not attall hard:
> Hee was a swapping, swapping mallard.
> Ho the blood etc.
>
> Hee was swapping all from bill to eye,
> Hee was swapping all from wing to Thigh;
> His swapping tool of Generation
> Oute swapped all ye winged Nation.
> Ho the blood etc.
>
> The lett us drink and dance a Galliard
> In ye Remembrance of ye Mallard,
> And as ye Mallard doth in Poole,
> Lett's dabble, dive and duck in Boule.
> Ho the bloud etc.

It is not certain which King Edward is meant, but it may be Edward VI, as the champion of Protestantism. The first verse refers to feasting, but the traditional foods eaten were pig, goose, capon rabbit and custard (rather than Bustard) and the turkey was first known in England in 1555.

In 1901 Cosmo Gordon Lang was Lord Mallard; he was chaired round the quadrangle for two hours by four Fellows, behind a dead mallard on a pole and senior Fellows carrying staves and torches which were piled up at the end to make a bonfire, before participants headed off to the Buttery to drink Madeira poured from a silver salt cellar shaped like a mallard, symbolically drinking the bird's blood.

In 2001 Dr Martin West took the role of Lord Mallard. Proceedings began with Evensong in the chapel, followed by drinks in Hall and a formal dinner for 120 people in the Library (the only room large enough), including female fellows for the first time, in black tie and academic dress. The menu was carefully selected and laid out to form the word 'Mallard'.

After the meal the company assembled in caps and gowns. A three-dimensional painted wooden mallard led the procession and Lord Mallard was chaired by six Fellows. Two Fellows carried poles surmounted by balls and crosses and others carried flaming torches. As they set off from the library Dr West sang a new verse of the song:

> Our famed Procession now appears:
> We do it every hundred years.
> We re-create the old effects,
> But this time plus a whole new sex.

The group processed round the Great Quad and the Front Quad, singing, and the more athletic climbed up the tower singing verses, while those in the quad sang the choruses. A fireworks display was held round a wooden mallard. A new medal was struck to commemorate the occasion with two ducks on the obverse to represent the fact that female Fellows took part in the event, and Christopher Wren's sundial on the reverse. The medal ribbons are in the college colours, yellow with a central red stripe.

Balliol College

Shepilinda's Memoirs, published in 1737, described Balliol Revels, held in the winter:

> This night all the young gay Striplings of the College are their own Masters, and no one can control them. Their custom is to stand at the gate and pick up whoever they meet (without regard either to sex, quality or age) and carry them into the Coll. Hall, and there, setting them astride upon a Brass Eagle that is in the middle of it, make them tell a story, and after that they generally make them very drunk. This sport lasts no longer than till nine o'clock, at which time the Master and tutors resume their wonted power.

There was often rivalry between colleges, and a Gordouli song was chanted over the wall from Balliol to Trinity College on drunken and celebratory occasions. The traditional words, according to Christopher Hibbert in *The Encyclopaedia of Oxford*, ran:

> Gordouli, Gordouli, Gordouli
> He's got a face like a ham
> Bobby Johnson says so
> And he ought to know.

The origin of this may have been when Robert Johnson, an exhibitioner at New College, dined at Balliol in 1896 and commented about a Trinity student nicknamed 'Gordouli' (after a firm manufacturing Egyptian cigarettes) that he had a 'face like a ham'. In fact the man, Arthur Mario Agniola Collier Galletti di Cadillac was very handsome. On hearing the Gordouli chant, Trinity men respond with:

> Balliol, Balliol,
> Bring out your black man
> [or bring out your white man]
> Jack Johnson says so
> And he ought to know.

This refers to a black heavyweight champion from 1908-15, Jack Johnson.

On Sunday evenings undergraduates spoon-bang on their tables as the Master walks to High Table, which is said to commemorate a Master who had been very ill returning to High Table after a long absence and the spoon-banging is in appreciation of his recovery.

Brasenose College

The College acquired its name from a brazen door knocker, which now hangs above the high table in the dining hall. It was taken by students migrating to Stamford in Lincolnshire in the fourteenth century and ended up as a front door knocker on a house which later became a girls' school. The school was purchased by Brasenose in 1890 to reclaim the knocker, but the college eventually made a substantial profit on the deal.

Each New Year's Day until the mid-eighteenth century all the undergraduates and Bachelors of Arts visited the Principal and gave him an epistle, wishing him a happy new year.

Brasenose undergraduates were given cakes and ale on Shrove Tuesday and ale verses were written and printed from 1709-89. A drink called Brasenose Ale or Lamb's Wool was served at dinner. The custom ceased in 1887, the year after the college bakehouse was demolished. Almonds, raisins ands figs were served at Good Friday dinner until the mid-eighteenth century.

Corpus Christi

The Mayor and Aldermen of Oxford processed annually in the eighteenth century to Corpus Christi to demand quit rent for their postern into the fields from the President.

Jesus College

This is a Welsh foundation, and on St David's Day college servants attached a green leek to the tassel of each member of the college's cap; this was worn to chapel and lectures until about 1875.

Magdalen College

On Commemoration days the college bells were rung in a 'confus'd manner' according to John Pointer, who, writing in 1749, described this as the 'primitive way of ringing'. On the first Monday in Lent the two Bursars gave out screws of paper containing two fourpenny pieces to Fellows and two pence to choristers.

During the Middle Ages May singing was done at several colleges, but Magdalen is the only one to have continued the tradition to the present day. It may have begun to greet the spring, or have had an ecclesiastical origin, (£10 was paid each year from the late seventeenth century to keep up vocals and music on the tower) but it probably began in 1509, when the tower was completed. The custom has changed and adapted over the centuries. In the eighteenth century a two hour concert of 'merry ketches' was held on top of the tower at four in the morning, followed by bell-ringing and breakfast for the participants. The hymn 'Te deum patrem colimus', (now known as 'Hymnus Eucharisticus') was written as a college grace by Thomas Smith, Fellow from 1666-92 and set to music by Benjamin Rogers, college organist and choirmaster from 1665-86, and was first used on May morning in the late eighteenth or early nineteenth century. The ceremony came into disrepute when choristers took rotten eggs up to the top of the tower and hurled them at those below, but in 1844 John Rouse Bloxam improved it by reinforcing the practice of the choir wearing surplices, ordering them to face East towards the sun as they sang, and making all participants remove their hats. In 1861 it became a Gaudy day and past Fellows and visitors were invited. Gradually it has become a Town and Gown event, and now after the singing the crowd massing on Magdalen Bridge rapidly disperses to enjoy varied entertainments, including morris dancing and refreshments on offer around the town.

Merton College

Regent's Fire or *Ignis Regentis,* last mentioned in 1514, was the occasion after supper in the Hall when a regent master entertained the masters and bachelors to a feast with wine, fire and amusements, to cheer them in the depths of winter.

Until 1686 it was customary for the Dean to keep Bachelor Fellows disputing for long hours in the hall, then give them a 'Black Night', in memory of a dispute between noted scholars Duns Scotus and William Occam, during which they raided the buttery and drank all night.

At Christmas in the eighteenth century the butcher employed by the Postmasters (Scholars) invited them for a treat at his house, providing a bull for the Steward to kill by knocking it on the head, known as the Kill-Bull.

May Morning at Magdalen College around 1910, with crowds massed below the tower. Photographed by Henry Taunt.

On the last night of the year, Scrutiny Night, all the college servants appeared in Hall after supper in front of the Warden and Fellows and offered them their keys. If they had committed any misdemeanour during the year their keys were taken away and they were dismissed, otherwise the keys were returned. Scrutiny days for Fellows were held on the eight days before Easter Day, Christmas and St Margaret's Day (10 June).

New College

Sometimes the Warden of New College made a progress, accompanied by a Fellow as Outrider, who guarded the cashbox from highwaymen, round the college lands, with picnics of chicken sandwiches and champagne. Alternatively college tenants were, in the eighteenth century, encouraged to pay their rents on time before Christmas by presenting all those who came with a pair of white gloves edged with red ribbons.

A chorister used to stand at the gate and summon members to dinner by shouting 'Eat-manchet-toat-serivat', a corruption of 'A mangervous, seigneurs' or 'A manger tous seigneurs'. A mallet was hit against the staircase to summon Fellows to quarterly college meetings, as at University College.

The Queen's College

The area in front of the college traditionally offered sanctuary from the Proctors, as did the area outside St John's College.

Robert de Eglesfield, who founded the college in 1341, decreed that scholars, most of whom came from Cumberland and Westmorland, should wear tabards, and eight senior students are still termed tabarders.

Celia Fiennes wrote in the seventeenth century:

> There is a very odd custom in Queen Coll. For every new-years-day there is a certain sum laid out in Needles and Thread which was left by the Founder, and every Gentleman of that Colledge has one given him with these words: 'Take this and be thrifty'.

The phrase 'needle and thread' or 'aiguille at fil' is a rebus of 'Robert de Eglesfield', a pious man, chaplain to Queen Philippa, who ordained that the Provost and twelve Fellows should wear crimson mantles symbolising the Blood of Christ, and they were to dine in Hall sat on one side of the High Table with the Provost opposite them in imitation of the Last Supper.

According to the *Oxford Times* of 7 January 1921 a dinner was held on New Year's night, with invited guests, and the Bursar presented each with a needle and thread, admonishing them to 'Take this and be thrifty'. There is a story that Prince Hal (later Henry V) was a student of the college, and his father Henry IV complained about the wastefulness of the college and his son's riotous behaviour. Hal was scolded by the Provost, and when he next saw his father had needles hanging from the eyelet holes of his doublet, to signify his new thrifty habits. In 1921 the Bursar approached each guest to enquire what type of degree he had, and gave needles threaded with blue silk thread to Doctors of Law, with black silk thread to Doctors of Divinity and with red thread to the others, with the traditional admonition and wishing them a happy new year. The guests attached the needles to the lapels of their gowns, leaving the threads hanging down. Jan Morris commented in 1965 that the custom had been moved to February.

The Boar's Head ceremony dates back to at least 1395/96, and is said to be in honour of the salvation of a scholar of The Queen's College named Copcot, who took his Greek text book up to Shotover, then a Royal hunting forest, to study. He was so engrossed in the text that he failed to notice a fierce wild boar bearing down on him until it was too late to run away or climb a tree. All he could think of doing was to thrust his book into the gaping jaws of the boar, which choked on it, gasping '*Graecum est!*' ('This is all Greek to me!') before expiring. Although this is a picturesque legend, it is more likely that the feast was held because the college was kept open at Christmas, as it was a long tedious journey home for many scholars, and the boar's head was a traditional Christmas dish. John Pointer wrote in 1749 that the boar's head, or a wooden effigy of one, was brought in with great solemnity on Christmas day. Taunt wrote in 1900 that the Hall was decked with evergreens, and a procession headed by the Provost, followed by Fellows walked through the hall to high table, where the Provost recited the College Grace. Then a trumpeter announced the entrance of a procession from the buttery, headed by the Tabarder chosen to sing the solo of the Boar's Head Carol, the choristers and the servitors carrying the boar's head on its silver salver on their shoulders. They sang as they processed up the hall and the Boar's Head was gently placed on high table, and embellishments, (probably flags and gilded sprigs of holly, mistletoe, rosemary and laurel) were removed and presented to choir boys and visitors, and the orange in the boar's mouth was given to the soloist.

The carol was already old when it was first published by Wynkin de Worde in 1521:

> The Boar's Head in hand bear I,
> Bedecked with bays and rosemary,
> And I pray you, my masters, be merry,
> Quot estis in convivio.
>
> Chorus: Caput apri defero,
> Reddens laudes Domino.
>
> The Boar's Head, as I understand,
> Is the rarest dish in all this land,
> Which thus bedecked with a gay garland
> Let us servire cantico,
>
> Chorus
>
> Our steward hath promised this,
> In honour of the King of Bliss,
> Which on this date to be served is,
> In reginensi atrio.
>
> Chorus

The Boar's Head ceremony at the Queen's College, showing the boar's head with its crown and flags being carried to high table.

During the two world wars when it proved impossible to obtain a boar's head a papier mâché one was used to keep up the tradition. In 1961 the ceremony was moved to the Saturday of the last week in the Christmas term.

John Pointer wrote in 1749 that the college gates were locked during dinner and supper lest the college be attacked again as it had been during the St Scholastica's Day riot when sixty-two students were injured.

St John's College

It was recorded in *Shepilinda's Memoirs* (1737) that:

> One day in the year the College Barber sings a song to the members called 'Adam Beck and Shuldledum and Midledum again the Drums beat thick and thick', but my informer could neither tell me the day that it is perform'd, nor the reason of this ancient custom.

Frumenty was served as refreshment in the middle of Lent until 1886. A candle, first lit on Christmas Eve, was lit over the twelve days of Christrmas in an ancient stone socket in the shape of the holy lamb, symbol of St John.

University College

Until 1864 the cooks here had a custom of 'chopping the block'. A tree decked with evergreens and flowers was set up on grass near the buttery and two cooks stood by it wearing white caps and jackets, one with a pewter plate to take the money and the other with the cleaver on a dish and every college resident chopped at the tree with the cleaver as he left Hall after dinner, each one putting money on the plate as a tip for the cook, the Master half a guinea and the Fellows five shillings and sixpence. Sometimes the 'tree' appears to have been a chopping block decorated with flowers.

BIBLIOGRAPHY

Alexander, S. *St Giles' Fair*, 1970
Allport, D.H. *Ramsden*, 1965
Aubrey, J. *MS Lansdowne*
Bailey, Robert C.S. *Hanborough*, 1927
Baker, M. *Folkore and Customs of Rural England*, 1974
Baker, J.H. *The Ipsden Country*, 1959
    The Story of the Chiltern Heathlands, 1932
Ballard, A. *Chronicles of the Royal Borough of Woodstock*, 1896
Bartlett, Alfred Durling, *Historical and Descriptive Account of Cumnor Place, Berkshire*, 1850
Beesley, A. *The History of Banbury*, 1841
Beesley, S. *My Life*, 1892
Beesley, T. *The Rollright Stones, Transactions of the Archaeological Society of North Oxfordshire 1853-55*
Belsen, M. *On The Press*, 2003
Bennett P., & Wilson, T. *The Old Stones of Rollright and District*, 1999
Berkshire Federation of Womens Institutes, *The Berkshire Book*, 1939
Berry, B. *Down the Green Groves*, 1989
Blair, J. *Anglo-Saxon Oxfordshire*, 1994
    St Frideswide Reconsidered, Oxoniensia 11, 1987
    Bampton Folklore, 2001
Bloxham, C. *May Day to Mummers*, 2002
    Portrait of Oxfordshire, Hale 1982
    The Book of Banbury, 1975
    The World of Flora Thompson, 1998
Bond, J. & Tiller, K. *Blenheim: Landscape for a Palace*, 1987
Bord, J & C. *Earth Rites*, 1982
    The Secret Country, 1976
Boss, Thomas Ward, *Reminiscences of Banbury*, 1903
Brabant, F.G. *Oxfordshire*, 1919
Brand, J. & Ellis, H. *Observations on the Popular Antiquities of Great Britain*, 1849
Briggs, K. *The Folklore of the Cotswolds*, 1974
    The Fairies in Tradition and Literature, 1967
Brody, A. *The English Mummers and their Plays*, 1970
Brown, Raymond Lamont, *Book of Superstitions*, 1970
Bruce Mitford, R.L.S. The Archaeology of the Bodleian Extension, Oxoniensia, Vol.IV, 1939
Burl, A. *The Rollright Stones*, 2000
Burns, J.S. *A History of Henley*, 1861
Burrows, M. *Collectanea*, 1890
    Worthies of All Souls, 1874
Carr, W. *University College*, 1902
Chandler, K. *Morris Dancing in the English South Midlands 1660-1900*, 1993
    Ribbons, Bells and Squeaking Fiddles, 1993

Cheetham, H. *Portrait of Oxford*, 1971
Churchwardens' Presentiments: Oxfordshire Archaeological Society, 1925
Claridge, J. *The Shepherd of Banbury's Rules to Judge the Changes of the Weather*, 1744
Clark, A. (ed.) *The Life and Times of Anthony Wood*, 1891
    The Colleges of Oxford, 1892
Clark, Walter H. *A Short History of Adderbury*, n.d.
Coleman, S. Jackson, *Tales and Traditions of Berkshire*, 1949
Colquhoun, I. *Pit, Pat the Pan's Hot*, 1975
Cooper, J. *White Horse Hill and Waylands Smithy*, 2000
Cooper, Jane & Smith, S. *The White Horse ands the Village of Uffington*, 2001
Coppock, G.A. and Hill, B.M. *Headington Quarry and Shotover*, 1933
Corbett, E. *A History of Spelsbury*, 1962
Cordrey, E. *Bygone Days at Iffley*, 1956
Crusha, Revd E.H.W. *May Day at Charlton-on-Otmoor*, 1977
Davison, Dorothy G.M. *The Story of Swalcliffe*, 1943
De Freitas, Leo John, *The Banbury Chapbooks*, 2004
Devereux, P. *Places of Power*, 1999
Disbury, D. & E. *The history of Ashbury Part I*, 1966
Ditchley, P.H. *Old English Customs Extant at the Present Time*, 1896
Dunkin, J. *History and Antiquities of the Hundred of Bullingdon and Ploughley*, Vol.1 and Vol.2,
    1823
    History of Bicester, 1816
Eddershaw, D. *The Civil War in Oxfordshire*, 1995
Ellis Davidson, H.E. 'Weland the Smith', *Folklore*, Vol.69. September 1958
    'Folklore and Man's Past', *Folklore*, Vol.74 Winter 1963
Emslie, J. Phillips, 'Scrape of Folklore', *Folklore*, Vol.26, 1915
Ettlinger, E. 'Folklore in Oxfordshire Churches', *Folklore*, Vol.73, August 1962
    'Documents of British Superstition in Oxford', *Folklore*, Vol.LIV, March 1943
Fisher, A. & Gerster, G. *The Art of the Maze*, 1990
Flick, P. 'The Rollright Stones', *Country Life*, August, 1973
Folk Music Journal, 1970
Gentleman's Magazine, the, 1866
Giles. J.A. *History of Bampton*, 1848
Green, A. *Our Haunted Kingdom*, 1973
Grinsell, Leslie V. *Folklore of Prehistoric Sites in Britain*, 1976
    The Rollright Stones and their Folklore, 1977
Groves, M.(ed.) *History of Shipton under Wychwood*, 1934
Gunther, R.T. *The Oxford Country*, 1912`
Hammond, N. *The White Horse Country*, 1972
Hardy. E.G. *Jesus College*, 1899
Hare, Augustus J.C. *The Years with Mother*, n.d.
Harris, M. *A Kind of Magic*, 1969
    The Green Years, 1976
Hassall, W.O. *Wheatley Records*, 1956
Hedges, S. *Bicester wuz a Little Town*, 1968
Helm. A. *The English Mummers' Play*, 1981
Henderson, Bernard W. *Merton College*, 1899
Hibbert, C. *The Encylopaedia of Oxford*, 1988
Hinton, D.A *Medieval Cistern from Churchill*, Oxoniensia Vol.XXXIII 1968
Hitching, F. *Earth Magic*, 1976
Hobhouse, C. *Oxford*, 1939
Hobson M.G. & Price, K.L.H. *Otmoor and its Seven Towns*, 1961
Hole, C. *British Folk Customs*, 1976
    English Folklore, 1945
    Haunted England, 1972
    MS Oxfordshire Collection
    'Some Folklore Survivals in English Domestic Life', *Folklore*, Vol.LXVIII, September 1957

Horn, P. *Oxfordshire Village Life: the Diaries of George James Dew*, 1983
    Country Life in the 1860s, 1986
Howard, A. *Endless Cavalcade*, 1964
Howkins, A. *Whitsun in nineteenth century Oxfordshire*, 1973
Hughes, T. *The Scouring of the White Horse*, 1859
Hudson, W.H. *The Illustrated Shepherd's Life*, 1987
Humphreys, Arthur L. *The Berkshire Book of Song, Rhyme and Steeple Chime*, 1935
Hurst, H. *Rambles Round Oxford*
Ingram, John H. The *Haunted House and Family Traditions of Great Britain*, 1928
Irving, J. *Stories from the History of Oxfordshire*, 1908
Jackson's *Oxford Journal*
Jenkins, S. *Discovering Minster Lovell*, 2000
Jessup, M. *A History of Oxfordshire*, 1975
Jewitt, C. Collectanea, *Folklore*, Vol.13, 1902
Judge, R. *The Jack in the Green*, 1979
    May Morning and Magdalen College, *Folklore*, Vol.97, 1986
Kibble, J. *Charming Charlbury*, 1930
    Historical and Other Notes on Wychwood Forest, 1928
    Historical and other notes on Charlbury, 1937
Kirtland, C. *Brief Memorials of the History of Chipping Norton*, 1871
Lamb, J. *Banbury Guardian*, April 1931
Lambrick, G. *The Rollright Stones*, 1988
Lester, E.R. *John Kalabergo of Banbury*, 1975
Linnard, W. 'The Shotover Giant', *Top*, Oxon, No.15, Winter 1970
Lockhart, J.C. *Cosmo Gordon Lang*, 1949
Macarthur, W. *The River Windrush*, 1946
Mais, S.B. *Our Village Today*, 1956
Malcolmson, R.W. *Popular Recreations in English Society*, 1973
Mallet, C.E. *History of the University of Oxford*, 1924
Manley, E.R. *A Descriptive Account of East Hendred*, 1969
Manning, Percy, MS *Top*. Oxon, Bodleian Library
    'Stray notes on Oxfordshire Folklore', *Folklore*, Vol.XIII, Sept 1902
    'Bringing in the Fly', *Folklore*, Vol.25, 1914
Massingham, J. *Chiltern Country*, 1942
Matthews, W.H. *Mazes, Labyrinths, their history and development*, 1970
Merrifield, R. *The Archaeology of Ritual and Magic*, 1987
Miller, E. *The History of the Village of Islip*, 1930
Miller, E. *The Forest Hill Village Book*, 1933
Millson, C. *Tales of Old Oxfordshire*, 1983
    Tales of Old Berkshire, 1977
Miles, D., Palmer S., Lock, G., Gosden C. & Cromarty, A.M. *Uffington White Horse and its*
    Landscape, 2003
Moreau, R.E. *The Departed Village*, 1968
Morris, A. Clifford, *The Rycote View*, 1978
Morris, C. *The Illustrated Journeys of Celia Fiennes*, 1982
Morris, J. *Oxford*, 1965
    The Oxford Book of Oxford, 1973
Muir, F. *Christmas Customs*, 1974
Northeast, P. *This Venerable Village*, 1975
Opie, I. & P. *Children's Games in Street and Playground*, 1969
    The Oxford Dictionary of Nursery Rhymes, 1951
Oxford Pageant Committee, *The Oxford Pageant*, 1907
Oxfordshire Archaeological Society Reports
Oxfordshire and District Folklore Society Annual Record
Oxfordshire Federation of Women's Institutes, *500 Jolly Good Things*, 1949
Parker, A. 'Oxfordshire Village Folklore', *Folklore*, Vol.34, 1923
Parker, J.H. *A Historical and Descriptive Account of Cumnor Place, Berks*, 1850

Parkes, G.D. & M. *May Day at Iffley*, 1934

Pearson, Edwin, *Banbury Chap Books*, 1890

Pickering, M. *Village Song and Culture*, 1982

Pimlott, J.A.R. *The Englishman's Christmas*, 1978

Plot, R. *Natural History of Oxfordshire* 1677

Plummer, A. & Early, R.E. *The Blanket Makers*, 1969

Pocock, E.A. *The Mystery of White Horse Hill*, 1968

Pointer, J. *Oxoniensis Academia or the Antiquities and Curiosities of the University of Oxford*, 1749

Ponsonby, Sir Charles, *Wootton: The Anatomy of an Oxfordshire Village 1945-1968*, 1968

Poole, Keith B. *Ghosts of Wessex*, 1076

Porter, E. *Cambridgeshire Customs and Folklore*, 1969

Potter. G.J.R. *Life in a Berkshire Village*, 1976

Potts, W. *Banbury Cross and the Rhyme*, 1930
    A History of Banbury, 1978

Powell, G.H. Stonesfield Through Two Centuries, MS

Prior, C.E. Transactions & Papers of the Oxfordshire Archaeological Society No.XL, Banbury, 1900
    Oxfordshire Archaeological Society Report for 1906

Prister Crutwell, M. *Ewelme: Its History and its People*, 1976

Pumphrey, C. *The Charlbury of our Childhood*, 1990

Quarrell, W.H. & W.J.C. (ed.) *Oxford in 1710 from the Travels of Zacharias Conrad von Uffenbach*, 1928

Quiller Couch, L. *Reminiscences of Oxford by Oxford Men*, 1892

Radford, E. & M.A. & Hole, C. *Encyclopaedia of Superstitions*, 1974

Readers Digest *Folklore Myths and Legends of Britain*, 1977

Reaney, B. *Class Struggle in Nineteenth Century Oxfordshire*, 1970

Richardson, J. *36 Strange Tales from Oxford and Shire*, 1981

Rix, M.B. *Boars Hill, Oxford*, 1970

Robins, D. *Circles of Silence*, 1985

Robins, F.W. *The Smith*, 1953

Rodgers, B. *Minster Lovell*, n.d.

Roud, S. *Mumming Plays in Oxfordshire: an interim checklist*, 1984

Roud, S. & Bee, M. *Berkshire Mumming Plays*, 1991

Rowell, G.A. 'Notes on some old-fashioned English Customs', *Folklore*, Vol.IV, 1886

Samuel, Raphael, (ed.) *Village Life and Labour*, 1973

Shilton: *A Village Scrapbook*, 1973

Sharp, C.J. & Macilwaine, H.C. *The Morris Book*, 1924

Smith, A.W. 'Some Folklore Elements in Movements of Social Protest', *Folklore*, Vol.77 pp 241-52, Winter 1966

Stanley Smith, M. Manuscript Notes, Oxfordshire Museum Store, Standlake

Stapleton, Mrs. *History of Kidlington, Yarnton and Begbroke*, n.d.

Steane, J. *Oxfordshire*, 1996

Steele, D. *Riding the Franchise*, 1991

Stewart, S. *Country Courtship*, 1975

Stonor, R.J. *Stonor*, 1951

Sturge Gretton, M. *A Corner of the Cotswolds*, 1914

Sturge Henderson, M. *Three Centuries in North Oxfordshire*, 1902

Surman, Phyllis, *Eliza of Otmoor*, 1975

Taunt, H.W. *The Boar's Head at Queen's College, Oxford*, n.d.

Taylor, L. & G. *Within Living Memory* [Headington], 1978

Thomas, K. *Religion and the Decline of Magic*, 1971

Thompson, F. *Lark Rise to Candleford*, 1945
    A Country Calendar, 1979

Tiddy, R.J.E. *The Mummers' Play*, 1923

Tongue, R.L. *Forgotten Folk Tales of the English Counties*, 1970

Turner, H. *Oxfordshire*, 1993

Turner, M.V. *The Story of Deddington*, 1931

Underwood, P. *Gazeteer of British Ghosts*, 1971

Vaux, Revd J.E. *Church Folklore*, 1894

Vincent, James E. *Highways and Byways of Berkshire*, 1931

Wakeling, G.H. 'History of the College 1603-10', Brasenose Quartercentenary Monographs, 1909

Weir, A. *Eleanor of Aquitaine*, 2000

Wells, W. *Journal of the English Folk Song and Dance Society* Vol.VIII, No.1, 1956

West, M. *The All Souls Mallard*, 2000

West Oxfordshire Oral History Broadsheet No.1

Wheeler, Peter M. *Beckley Reflects*, 1999

Williams, A. *Villages of the White Horse*, 1913

   Folk Songs of the Upper Thames, 1923

Williams, E.C. *Companion into Oxfordshire*, 1944

Williams Mr., Minster Lovell Notebooks, typescript, *c.* 1930

Wing, W. *The Antiquities and History of Steeple Aston*

Wise, P. & S. *About Burford*, 1976

Wodhams, J.R. *The Midland Garner*, 1882

Wood, A. *History and Antiquities of the University of Oxford*, 1674

Wordsworth, C. *Social Life at the English Universities*, 1874

Wright, A.R. & Lones, T.E. *British Calendar Customs*, 1936

Yarrow, I. *Berkshire*, 1952

INDEX

Abingdon 6, 26, 30, 35, 52, 54, 65, 113, 124, 125, 126, 127, 128, 130, 133, 136, 138, 141, 165, 185
Abingdon bun throwing 124
Abingdon mummers 133, 136, 185
Abingdon Traditional Morris Men 6, 128, 185
Ackington Way 155, 185
Adderbury 100, 103, 123, 126, 133, 138, 143, 144, 146, 155, 165, 181
Advent 136
Adwell Cop 139
Albert, Prince 123
Albury 56, 57
Alexandra, Queen 98
Alf Balls' Wild West Show 121
Alfred, King 115, 133, 157
Algar, King 24, 25
All Souls College 6, 169, 171, 181, 184
Allen, James 41
Allied Carpets 135
Ambrosden 55, 66, 112, 143, 148
Ancient Order of Foresters 118
Anglo-Saxons 13, 16, 24, 25, 26, 27, 92, 145, 180, 185
animals 17, 32, 45, 96, 141
Appleford 42, 94
April Fool 108
Archbishop's Maze 21
archery 84
Ardington 15, 115
Ardley 71
Ascension 53, 93
Ascott-under-Wychwood 43, 108, 132, 140

Ash Wednesday 81, 93, 106
Ashbury 15,, 19, 181
Ashdown, Battle of 16, 18
Ashfield, Miss 63
Ashmolean Museum 26
Asthall Leigh 132
Aston Rowant 67, 101
Aston Upthorpe 15
Atkins, Squire 26
Atrebates 16
Aubrey, John 16, 56, 90, 99, 107, 123, 180
Augustinian canons 24
Aunt Sally 87, 88

backswording 85, 86, 87, 122
Badger baiting 84
Baker, J.H. 139, 180
ball games 106, 107, 108
Baldons, the 106
Balliol College 173, 174
Balliol Revels 173
Balscote 54
Banbury 48, 69, 160, 161, 162, 163, 182, 183, 185, 186, 188
Banbury cakes 48, 162
Banbury Co-operative and Industrial Society 163
Banbury crosses 160, 161, 162
Banbury Guardian 69, 182
Barford St Michael 50
Barnard Gate 145
Barton Lane, Headington 153
Barton Park 12
Bartons, the 110, 134
Baskerville, Thomas 17
Baynard's Green 146
Beach, Mrs 153

beating the bounds 53
Beckley 13, 38, 46, 94, 99, 152, 154, 184
Beesley, Alfred 144, 180
Begbroke 68, 184
Bellarmine, Cardinal 78
bells 125, 135, 156, 159, 160, 161, 164, 175, 181
Benedictine monks 150
Benson 22, 143
Berrick Salome 72, 88, 94, 97
Beth-oni 153
Bicester 9, 46, 51, 60, 68, 69, 70, 76, 78, 84, 85, 89, 90, 92, 96, 112, 114, 118, 124, 125, 133, 141, 145, 148, 157, 181, 185, 187
Bicester Priory 92
Bicester wuz a Little Town 89, 181
Binney, E.H. 134
birds 14, 50, 62, 80, 83, 94, 96, 97, 107, 121, 140
birth 54, 55, 97, 111, 124, 136
Bisham 94
black dog 39, 145, 153
Black Night 175
Black Prince, Woodstock 120
Blacksmith 73, 76, 89, 153
Blackthorn 74, 112, 143
Blenheim Palace 11, 12, 21, 120, 180
Blenheim, Woodstock etc. 11, 12
Bletchingdon 107
Blount, Janet 165
Blowing Stone 26
Bloxam, John Rouse 175
Bloxham 51, 52, 80, 113, 133, 143, 144, 155, 156

Bloxham, John 156
Boar's Head ceremony 177, 178, 179, 184
Bodicote 104, 105
Bodleian Library 6, 13, 79, 180, 182
Bonfire Night 122, 168
Boer War 96
Bosworth, Battle of 34
Botley 133
Bowden, Sir Frank and Lady 66
Bowers, Harriet 65
Bowers, Sarey 142, 185
Bowers, William 185
Boxing Day 123, 124, 126
Boy Bishops 169
Brasenose Ale 184, 185
Brasenose College 168, 174, 184
Bride 34, 35, 58, 59, 60,m 84, 129
Briggs, Katharine 140, 180
Brighthampton 13
Brightwell Baldwin 41, 63, 186, 134, 137
Brightwell-cum-Sotwell 155
Brill 46
Britannia Inn, Headington 131
Brize Norton 115
Brokenbarrow 13
Bronze Age 8, 13, 15, 16, 20, 139
Broughton Castle 37, 38, 160
Bruern 148
Bruern Abbey 148
Brunner, Lady 21, 22
Buckingham 55
Buckinghamshire 23
Buckland 26
Buckland, Mother 141
Bucknell 133
Bucknell Manor 133
builders 74, 78
bull baiting 84, 85
Bull of Banbury 163
Burcote, Prudence 150
Burford 39, 42, 43, 44, 47, 61, 104, 115, 117, 118, 122, 125, 132, 136, 146, 147, 148, 154, 186
Burford Bridge 47, 186
Burford dragon 6, 117, 118, 136
Burford Priory 146
Burford School 117
burial 13, 16, 54, 61, 62, 66, 146

Butcher's Row, Banbury 160
Butler, Dick 130

Cadillac, Arthur di 174
Calendar of Oxford Quarter Sessions 141
Cam, Betty 141
candle auctions 68
Candlemass 67, 68, 95, 105, 170
Canterbury, Archbishop of 21, 22, 24
Canute, King 27
Capewell, Mrs 51
Capping out 74
Capps Lodge 42
Cardus, Kenneth 52
carol singing 123
carters 72, 85, 120, 142
Cary, Lucius, Lord Falkland 39
Cassington 165
Castle, William (Old Mettle) 135 186
Catesby, Sir William 34
Cattern Morris 133
Chadlington 146
Chagford 23
Chalgrove 38, 107, 146
Chancellor's Court 168
Chancery, Court of 27
Chandler, Keith 6, 126, 181
Chantilly 160
Charlbury 49, 74, 81, 83, 84, 100, 101, 115, 123, 138, 155, 156, 158, 182, 183
Charlbury Flitch 83
Charles I 37, 38, 39, 45, 141
Charles II 39, 42, 109, 111, 125
Charlton-on-Otmoor 46, 51, 72, 93, 111, 181
Charlton-on-Otmoor Primary School 113
Chastleton 19, 39, 40, 101
Chastleton House 39, 40
Checkendon 143, 148
Chesterfield, Roger de 167
childhood 54, 183
children's games 88, 89,, 90, 91
Childrey 86
Chilson 108
Chilswell 94
Chilsworth 72
chimney 34, 60, 62, 74, 79, 109, 144
chimney sweep 60, 109
Chinnor 13, 38, 138, 143
Chipping Norton 8, 12, 41, 42, 61, 79, 95, 106, 148, 153, 182

Chopping the Block 179
Christchurch Cathedral 25
christening 54, 55, 56, 79, 95
Christmas 34, 57, 67, 77, 83, 94, 95, 104, 105, 122, 123, 124, 133, 135, 136, 137, 165, 169, 170, 171, 175, 176, 177, 179
Christmas kings 169, 170
church bells 51, 63, 68, 102, 104, 106, 159, 164
Church Hanborough 148
Church leads 52
Churchill 46, 79, 132, 182
churching 56
Churchwardens 52, 54, 107, 108, 113, 125, 126, 181, 186
Churchwardens' Presentiments 181, 186
Churn Knob 23
Clarence, Duke of 66
Clattercote 100
Clifford, Rosamund 30,31
Clifton 158
Clifton Hampden 148, 151, 153
Clipping the Church 107
Club Feasts 117, 129
Coate, Randall 21
Cobb, Sir George 103, 146
cobbler 77, 128
cock-fighting 84, 114
Cogges 136, 158
Cogges Manor Farm 136
Coker, John 85
Collins, Joe 39
Colwell Spring 94
Commemoration Days 175
Commonwealth 39, 109, 170
Condive's Corner 49
Convocation 168
Cook, Mr 52
Copcot 177
Coppock, G.A. 90, 181
Corbet, Elsie 95, 181
Cork, Job 15
Corn Exchange, Oxford 131
Cornbury Park 36
Corpus Christi College 171, 174
Cottisford 70
Country Calendar, the 74, 184
Country Courtship 106, 184
Country Life 160, 181
'Courtiers', Clifton Hampden 151

courtship 56, 105
Coventry Museum 15
Cowper, William 34
Cracklow, Elizabeth 100
Crake, Revd Edward 15, 152
Cranstoun, Captain Willliam 150, 151
Crawley 115, 158
cricket 61, 75, 119, 145, 155
Croke, Sir Alexander 45
Cromwell, Oliver 20, 38, 39, 71
crossroads 12, 49, 65
Crouch Hill, Banbury 143, 144
Crowell 22, 93
Crowmarsh 15
Croydon, John de 167
Crusha, Revd E.H.D. 46, 181
Cuckhamsley 13
cuckoo pens 22
cudgel-playing 85, 86
Culham 70
Culpeper, Jane 148
Cumberland 177
Cumnor 35, 36, 180, 183
Cumnor Place 35, 36, 180, 183
Cuthbert, King 117
Cuthred, King 117
Cynegils, King 23

Dalby 20, 35
Danes 16, 25, 26, 27
Daniels, Bill 137
Dashwood family 133
Davies, Revd Henry 52
Davis, Richard 100
Dean 155
death 54, 58, 61, 62, 63, 65, 66, 68, 74, 95
death omens 36, 61, 62, 97
Deddington 48, 84, 95, 121, 159, 184
Deddington Pudding Pies 48
Delafield 139
deposits in buildings 79
Devil, the 10, 11, 13, 15, 39, 43, 51, 63, 67, 80, 83, 105, 107, 134, 136, 141, 143, 144, 145
Devil's Corner 145
Devil's Churchyard 143
Devil's Punchbowl 143
Devil's Quoits 11
Dew, Dorothy 91
Dew, George James 142, 182

Dew, Philip 'Philly' 130
Didan, king 24
Didcot 97, 153
Ditchley 12, 36, 88
divinations 39, 56, 57
Divinity School 169, 170, 177
Dixey, George 130
Dobunni 16
Dorchester Abbey 24, 51, 148, 151, 187
Dorchester-on-Thames 23, 24, 51, 94, 146, 148, 151
Dorham, Letys 141
Dragon Hill 16, 17, 18
Dragon Hoard 13
Drake, Miss 139
Drayton 54, 101, 134, 138
Drayton St Leonard 53
Ducklington 56, 57, 70, 71, 80, 81, 88, 90, 91, 97, 101, 102, 103, 115, 132, 133, 138, 155, 158, 166
Ducklington moonrakers 166
Dudley, Lady Lettice 36
Dudley, Sir Robert 35, 36, 37, 150
Dunkin, J. 85, 112, 124, 181
Dunsden Brothers 42
Durham College 79
Duval, Claude 41
Dyers City Livery Company 98, 99
Dynevore, Lord 44

Early's blanket factory 75, 183
East End public houses 157
East Hendred 13, 148, 156
Easter 83, 93, 95, 106, 107, 108, 176
Edgehill, Battle of 37, 38
Edgington, David 126, 130
Edmund Ironside, King 27
Edward the Confessor 27, 28, 93
Edward III 79, 167
Edward VI 172
egg rolling 107
Eglesfield, Robert de 177
Eldridge, 65
Eleanor of Aquitaine 30, 31
Eleanor of Provence 31
Elizabeth I 35, 45, 115
Elizabeth, HRH the Queen Mother 124
Elsfield 79, 154
Encaenia 168, 169
Encyclopaedia of Oxford 173, 181

Enstone 12, 49, 113, 154, 157
Enstone public houses 157
Ethelbald, King 117
evergreens 60, 105, 109, 111, 112, 113, 119, 123, 177, 179
Ewelme 22, 40, 80, 81, 82, 83, 148, 165
Eynsham 6, 60, 80, 81, 82, 83, 117, 132, 133, 145, 148, 165
Eynsham morris 132
Eynsham Poaching Song 165
Exmoor 23

fairies 56, 139, 180
fairs 48, 120, 121, 160
Faringdon 26, 138, 152
farming 67, 71, 104
Fawler 49, 158
Fawley 49
Ferry Hinksey 101
Fettiplace family 154
Field Assarts 132
Field Town 156
Fiennes, Celia 160, 177, 183
Fiennes, Nathaniel 160
Fifield 42
Filkins 58, 68, 85, 88, 96, 117
Finstock 80, 115, 132, 133, 138, 146, 158
First World War 10, 96, 109, 122, 153
Fisher, Adrian 21, 181
Fletcher, Captain 151
Fletcher, Sarah 151
Flibbertigibbet 14, 15
flowers 62, 63, 64, 65, 91, 92, 93, 99, 109, 113, 129, 130, 179
Folklore of the Cotswolds, The 140, 180
Folk medicine 100, 102, 103
folk songs 71, 77, 164, 165
Folk Songs of the Upper Thames 77, 184
food and drink 18, 82, 83
Forest Hill 60, 68, 95, 102, 103, 182
Forster, Anthony 35
Fothergill Robinson, Revd W. 80
Frederick William, Prince of Prussia 160
Freeland 61, 73, 83
Freemen of Oxford 68, 119
freshmen rituals 170

Fringford Mill 139, 140
Froggledown Lane 38
Frogley's Farm, Bicester 38
Frumenty 179
Fryer, Major Francis 127
Fulbrook 42, 155
funerals 52, 63, 64, 100

Gabriel Hounds 146
Gage's Boxing Booth 121
Gainfield 26
Galloway, Mother 142
Gammer Gurton's Garland 159
Garsington 13, 65, 142
George III 124
George IV 124
George Inn, Wallingford 40
ghosts 122, 145, 147, 148, 150, 153, 183, 184
Giant's Grave, Shotover 20
Giant's marbles 19
Gibbons, Grinling 21
Giles, Dr. 137, 181
Gillet, Thomas 19
gleaning 70
Gloucester City Morris Men 118
gloves 42, 48, 64, 79, 80, 81, 105, 171, 176
goblin 49, 139
Godstow 31, 32
Godstow Nunnery 31, 32, 68
Gomme, Sam 46
Good Friday 62, 67, 77, 81, 82, 100, 107, 174
Good Friday loaf 82
Gordouli 173, 174
Goring 30, 49, 94, 101
Grafton 71
Gravenhill 145
Graves, Robert 46
Great Milton 54, 153
Great Tew 88, 89, 90, 94, 102, 146, 148, 154
Green Man 51
Gregory, Elizabeth 141
Greys Court 21, 22, 35
Grim's Ditches 15
groaning cakes 187
Gunnington, P.A.V. 63
Gunther, Anne 141
Gurden, George 141
Guy Fawkes Night 122
gypsies 65, 84

Hailey 115, 158
Hall, Ann 153

Hall, Thomas 153
halloween 57, 122, 170
Hamilton, Captain, 46
Hampden, John 148
Hanborough 38, 57, 61, 64, 70, 87, 137, 148, 158, 180
Hanwell 73, 151
Hanwell Castle 151
Harcourt family 11, 65, 152
Hare, Augustus 152
hares 43, 82, 165
Hart St, Henley-on-Thames 151
harvest 52, 59, 67, 68, 70, 71, 95, 97, 140
Hatford 26
Hawes, Phoebe 141
Headington 20, 52, 54, 66, 74, 84, 90, 97, 119, 122, 131, 141, 153
Headington Quarry 59, 63, 117, 131, 133, 134, 135, 136, 137, 138, 181, 184
Headington Quarry Morris Men and Mummers 6, 59, 126, 131, 133, 134, 135, 136
Hedges, Sid 89, 145, 157, 181
Hemmings family 127, 128, 188
Hempton 159
Hendreds, the 13, 15, 133, 148, 153, 156
Hengist 16, 17
Henley-on-Thames 22, 35, 49, 52, 99, 108, 113, 123, 150, 151, 155, 180
Henry I 119
Henry II 30, 31, 32, 119, 167
Henry III 31, 79
Henry IV 177
Henry V 177
Henry VI 149
Henry, son of Simeon 167
herbal medicine 100, 101, 140
Heron, Cecily 150
Heywood, Jason 170
Hibbert, Christopher 173, 181
Hibbert, Colonel 133
Higden, Ranulf 31, 32
highwaymen 7, 41, 146, 176
Hill, Mary 49
Hind, James 41, 42
Hinksey 25, 101, 144
Hinksey Manor 144
History and Antiquities of the University of Oxford 170, 184

History of Banbury 28, 37, 144, 180
History of Spelsbury 95, 181
Hoar Stones 9, 12
Hole, Christina 6, 139
Holy Innocents' Day 169
holy wells 92
Holton 60
Hock Monday and Tuesday 108
Honorius, Pope 23
Hopcroft's Holt 12, 41
Hood, Robin 28, 29, 52, 113, 115, 137
Hook Norton 103, 153, 156
Hook Norton Public Houses 156
hoops 88, 89, 110, 123
Horley 146
Horley, Tom 142
Horne, Elizabeth 141
Horsa 16
horsemen 72, 73, 145
horseshoes 73, 142
household superstitions 81
Hugh, Bishop of Lincoln, 31
Hughes, Thomas 6, 18, 86, 87, 182
Hunt, Ted 137
Hunting the Mallard 172, 173
Hutchins family 72

Icknield Way 15, 133
Idbury 22, 132
Iffley 50, 59, 63, 64, 65, 110, 111, 123, 136, 181, 183
Infant Institutes… 159
Inspecting the City Walls 108
Ipsden 22, 143, 144, 180
Iron Age 13, 15, 16, 18, 92, 143
Iron Well 93
Isaacs, Sam 65
Iseult 31
Islip 27, 28, 46, 73, 74, 83, 133, 136, 137, 182
Islip Bridge, Battle of 39

Jack in the Green 109, 182
jack-o'-lantern 139
Jackson, Miss 51
Jackson, Mrs 51
Jackson, Stuart 127
Jackson's Oxford Journal 65, 86, 121
Jagger, James 141
James I 122, 141, 146

James II 100
James, Rod 136
Jeffries, Judge 27
Jenny Newton's Well 94
Jesus College 175, 181
jingling 18, 87
John, King 28
Johnson, Jack 174
Johnson, Robert 174
Jones, Arthur 39, 40
Jones, Charlie 59
Jones, Sarah 39
Joseph's Stone 13
Juniper Hill 164

Kalabergo, John 45, 46, 47, 48, 182
Kalabergo, William 48
Katharine of Aragon 92
Kelmscott 80, 81
Kencot 94, 104
Kenilworth 14
Kennington 61
Kibble, John 80, 102, 103, 142, 157, 182
Kidlington 55, 80, 107, 115, 155, 184
Kidlington Lamb Ale 115
Kimber, Arthur 59
Kimber, William 59, 131
King Alfred's School 26
King's Evil 100
King of the Beans 170
King Stone 8, 9, 10, 11, 139
Kingham 65, 88
Kings Sutton 143
Kingston Lisle 26, 94
Kirtlington 82, 97, 115, 116, 117, 125, 133, 134, 141, 142
Kirtlington Lamb Ale 115, 116, 117
Kirltlington Park 133
knives 82, 96, 142

Lacy family 154
Lamb Ales 115, 116, 117, 133
Lamb, Joshua 69, 72
Lambrick, George 8, 182
Lang, Cosmo Gordon 173, 182
Langford 132
Lark Rise to Candleford 6, 70, 90, 184
Laud, Archbishop 37, 85
Launton 81, 123
Leach, Henry 165

Leafield 61, 93, 115, 132, 133, 146, 153
Leland, John 32
Lent 27, 48, 59, 106, 107, 175, 179
Leowin 25
leprosy 100
Letcombe Basset 143
Lidstone 12, 79
Lincoln College 53, 63
Lindsay, Lord and Lady 115
Little Tew 153, 154
Little, Thomas 114
Littlemore 108
Littleworth 20
Lockinge 115, 136
London 23, 31, 41, 42, 61, 73, 99, 141, 154
Long Compton 9
Long Crendon 131
Long Hanborough 64, 70, 137
Long Wittenham 133
Lord Churchill's Yeomanry 46
Lord of Misrule 170
Louis VII 167
Lovell, Francis Lord 33, 34
Lower Heyford 53, 56, 63, 81, 88, 89, 91, 102, 142
Lupercalia 105
Lyneham 12

Magdalen College 93, 169, 175, 176, 182
Magpie Lane, Oxford 150
Manning, Percy 6, 114, 131, 182
Mapledurham Treasure 23
marbles 19,, 88, 89, 187
Markets 26, 43, 61, 76, 78, 85, 124, 160, 161, 168
Marlborough, 1st Duke of 128
marriage 61, 24, 54, 56, 58, 60, 88, 106, 150, 160
Marsh Bridge, Didcot 153
Martin, Canon R.R. 180
Matilda, Queen 30
May Day 6, 7, 93, 108, 109, 110, 112, 160, 180, 181, 183
May games 109
maypoles 109, 111, 113, 114, 116, 160
mazes 21, 22, 30, 31, 181, 182
Meacock, James 100
Merlin 11, 19
Merchant Tailors, Guild of 117

Merton 145
Merton College 170, 175, 181
Michaelmas 68, 71, 91
Middleton Stoney 27, 28, 159
Midland Garner, the 68, 104
Mid Deus Sunday 106
Middle Aston 139
midsummer 9, 12, 117, 136, 139
Miller of Mansfield Inn 30
millers 30, 73, 165
Milton 44, 105, 131, 139
Milton, John 139
Milton-under-Wychwood 132, 142
Minster Lovell 33, 34, 35, 62, 67, 94, 132, 164, 182, 183, 184
Miserere Mei Sunday 106
Mistletoe Bough 34, 35, 123
Mock Mayors 119, 120, 127, 128
Mollington 166
Mollington moonrakers 166
More, Sir Thomas 150
Moreau, R.E. 62, 156, 182
Moreland's Theatricals 121
Moreton 87, 133
morris dancing 6, 7, 68, 125, 126, 127, 129, 131, 133, 135, 137, 175, 181
Morris, James 168
Mortimer, John 102
Mother's Day 106, 107
mummers 5, 6, 7, 125, 127, 129, 131, 132, 133, 134, 135, 136, 137, 180, 181
Musee Conde 189

Napier coach 146
Napier, Sir George 146
Natural History of Oxfordshire 74, 183
Neal, Mrs 51
Needle and Thread ceremony 177
Neolithic 8, 12, 113, 16, 20, 92
Nether Worton 53
New College 93, 108, 131, 169, 170, 174, 176
New Yatt 145
New Year 9, 62, 104, 108, 170, 174, 177
Noke 46, 9, 145
North Aston 64
North Hinksey 144

North Leigh 57, 62, 64, 66,
    80, 81, 82, 83, 96, 100,
    103, 132, 133, 142, 145,
    153, 165, 166
North Moreton 133
Northampton, Earl of 39
Northumberland 135
Northmoor 107, 154
November 5th 122, 168
Nuffield 15
Nuney Green 139
nutting 54, 128, 130, 145

Oak Apple Day 111, 113
Occam, William 175
Ock Street, Abingdon 126,
    127, 128
Oddfellows 117, 131
Oddington 45, 46, 93
Old Headington 66, 119
Old Marston 108
'Old Mettle' (William Castle)
    133
Old Moll Well 94
Oldys, Dr 40
omens 54, 58, 61, 62
On the Press 77
Opie, Iona and Peter 88, 183
Otmoor 7, 13, 45, 46, 51, 72,
    93, 111, 112, 113, 146,
    181, 182
Otmoor riots 146, 181, 182
Owen, Mrs. 35
Oxford 6, 7, 19, 24, 25, 30, 33,
    36, 38, 41, 42, 43, 44, 46,
    48, 53, 61, 63, 64, 65, 68,
    73, 74, 77, 79, 81, 84, 88,
    90, 92, 93, 94, 96, 101,
    103, 107, 108, 109, 116,
    119, 121, 122, 123, 130,
    131, 132, 141, 143, 146,
    150, 154, 166, 167, 173,
    174, 181, 182
Oxford Castle 30
Oxford City Morris Men 133
Oxford Journal 61
Oxford Pageant 6, 25, 30,
    36, 168
Oxford Prison 46
Oxford Times 61, 177
Oxford University Press 77
Oxfordshire Museums Service
    64
Oxfordshire Yeomanry 46

Palm Sunday 83, 93, 106, 107
Parker, Angelina 70, 183

Passion Sunday 106
Penda, King of Mercia 92
Penfold, Frederick 63
Pepplewell, Agnes 141
Pentecost 33
Percy's Reliques 32
personal superstitions 80
Pewse, Wyllyam 27
phantom hitch-hiker 146,
    148, 153
Philippa, Queen 177
Phillips, Jim 59
Phipps, John 54
Piddington 21, 64
Pitt, Beryl 59
Pitt Rivers Museum 6, 101,
    116
plant lore 99
Plot, Dr R. 74, 84, 93, 117,
    183
Plough Monday 67
Plough Sunday 67
poaching 7, 4, 3, 44, 45, 165
Pointer, John 175, 177, 179,
    183
Pole, Alice de la 149
Pole, William de la 149
Pope, Alan 108
Pope's Tower 152
Port Meadow 68
postmasters 175
Powell, G.H. 62, 183
Project Merlin 11
pub games 87, 88
Pullin, Ann 189
puritans 84, 109, 113, 125,
    160
Pusey 27
Pusey horn 27
Pye, Hampden 152

Queen Anne 91, 99
Queen Caroline 91
Queen Emma's Morris 133
Queen's College, the 176,
    177, 178
Quiet Woman, the 41
Quill winders 75
Quintain 82, 115
quoits 88

rabbits 43, 97, 139, 172
races 17, 18, 68, 88
Rackham's Lane, Oxford 143
Radband, Harry 'Sarah' 189
Radband, Robert 137
Radley 107

Ramsden 65, 146, 156, 158
Ratcliffe, Sir William 34
Rawlinson, Dr. 93
Reading Mercury 17
Reeves, Jonas 141
Reformation 24, 50, 52, 92,
    105, 106, 111, 169
Reindeer Inn, Banbury 78
Remains of Gentilisme 56
Rex Fabarum 170
rheumatism 102
Richard III 33, 34
Ridgeway 13, 15, 17
Riding the Franchise 108, 184
Risinghurst 108
Ritson, Joseph 159
roads 12, 14, 15, 26, 38, 40,
    41, 48, 49, 56, 65, 79,
    84, 85, 88, 91, 93, 100,
    102, 153
Robsart, Amy 35, 36
Rochester, Lord 40, 41
Rogers, Benjamin 175
Rollright Stones 7, 8, 9, 10,
    11, 139,, 140, 180, 181
Roman 13, 20, 23, 28, 59,
    100, 101, 105, 140, 145,
    172
Roman soldier ghost 145
Rookery Pond, Bicester 148
Rose and Crown, Woodstock
    119, 120, 141
Rotherfield Greys 70
Rough Music 60, 61
Rouse, Mary Ellen 142
Rouse, Joe 130
Rouse, Terry 137
Rowland, Margaret 42
Rumbold, Stephen 41
Runcie, Robert, Archbishop of
    Canterbury 22
Rupert, Prince 38
Rush strewing 52
Russell, Miriam 141
Rycote 94, 150, 183

Safrida 24
St Andrew's Day 122
St Anthony's well 94
St Bartholomew's Chapel 93
St Birinus 23, 24
St Blaise 74
St David's Day 175
St Edburg 92
St Edmund Hall 93
St Frideswide 24, 25, 92, 180
St George 16, 18, 133

St Giles' Fair 83, 121, 170, 180
St John the Baptist 117
St John's College, Oxford 37, 170, 176, 179
St Margaret's church 143, 176
St Margaret's well 92, 93
St Mark's Eve 61
St Martin's church, Oxford 167
St Mary's church, Oxford 25, 36, 37, 64, 168
St Mary's church, Warwick 37
St Mary the Virgin 36, 167, 169
St Michael-at-the-Northgate, Oxford 53, 74
St Nicholas' Day 169
St Peter's Day 68
St Scholastica's Day 167, 168, 179
St Stephen's Day 123, 124
St Swithun's Day 83, 95
St Valentine 105, 106
Sandford-on-Thames 38, 65, 46
Sanger, George 121
Sarsden 27
Saxton, Edward 120
Saye and Sele, Lord 37, 38
Saunders, Mrs 141
Scarve, John 144
Scott, Sir Walter 14
Scotus, Duns 175
Scouring of the White Horse, the 6, 17, 18, 20, 86, 87, 182
Scrivener, Mrs Thomas 89
Scrutiny Night 176
Searle, Revd Philip 45
Second World War 11, 18, 20, 148
Shakespeare, William 139
Shaking Charlotte 142
Sharp, Cecil 129, 131, 183
Sharp, Giles 39
sheep 19, 49, 60, 62, 72, 94, 101, 103, 121, 142, 148
Sheldonian Theatre 169
Shenington 52
Shepherd of Banbury 94
Shepilinda's Memoirs 173, 179
shepherds 15, 27, 62, 71, 72, 94, 96, 101, 123, 148, 157, 182
Sheriff of Oxford 68, 108
Shick-shack day 111
Shifford 158

Shillingford 56, 98
Shilton 165, 183
Shipton Manor 190
Shipton-under-Wychwood 9, 12, 43, 63, 65, 72, 131, 159, 181
Shirburn 22
Shistawi, Ahmed 136
shoes 25, 42, 53, 54, 73, 79, 81, 87, 152, 160
Shotover 19, 20, 42, 43, 60, 90, 94, 107, 181, 197
Shotover Giant 19, 182
Shrivenham 154
Shrove Tuesday 52, 75, 106, 170, 174
Sibford 69, 72
Sicily, Kings of 31
Simnel, Lambert 34
sin eating 66
Singer's Royal Wax Works 121
Sinodun Hills 22
skipping 88, 89
Smith, Mrs Jack 51
Smith, Matilda 65
Smith, Thomas 175
Smith, William Edmund Morley 60
Smithett, Enid 11
smock funerals 64
Snivelling Corner 15
Snow, Mr 141
Somerton 6, 20, 21, 63, 64, 125
Sotwell 134, 137, 155, 186
Souldern 136, 142, 158
South Leigh 54
Sparks family 157
spectral coaches 146
Spelsbury 12, 35, 49, 56, 58, 76, 81, 93, 94, 95, 97, 101, 132, 142, 146, 155, 181
spoon banging 174
sporting the oak 171
sports 5, 84, 85, 87, 89, 91, 114, 117, 122
Springheuse, Walter de 167
Stamford 174
standing stones 12
Standlake 13, 102, 103, 154, 184
Stanford 174
Stanton Harcourt 11, 65, 92, 132, 152, 154
Star Chamber, the 141
Steeple Aston 64, 155, 184

Steeple Barton 97, 141
Stephen, King 190
Steventon 133
Stewart, Sheila 105, 184
Stoke 60, 155
Stoke, Battle of 34
Stoke Lyne 141
Stoke Row 61, 82, 88, 139
Stonesfield 62, 73, 156, 158, 183
Stonesfield Through the Ages 183
Story of the Chiltern Hundreds, the 139, 180
Stow-on-the-Wold 68
Stowford Farm, Barton 141
Stratton Audley 56, 95, 105
Streatley 15
Strowell 93
Student customs 170
Studley Priory 111
Stukeley 8
suicides 35, 49, 65, 148, 151, 153
Sunningwell 94, 136
superstitions 54, 63, 67, 71, 78, 80, 81, 82, 180
Sutton 154
Sutton Courtenay 133, 134
Swalcliffe 68, 123, 181
swans 6, 98, 99, 157, 172
Swan Upping 6, 98, 99
sweeps' procession 109
Swinford, George 58, 88
sword dance 125, 128, 129, 135
Swyncombe 22

Tackley 72, 153, 166
Tadmarton 21, 68
Tadmarton Heath 21
Tandy, Revd 48
Tanfield, Lord and Lady 39, 146, 147, 148
Tangley Hall 42, 148
Tanner, Jim 130
Tanner, Tom 130
tar barrels 102, 122
Taston 13, 155
Taunt, Henry 11, 12, 109, 110, 111, 176, 177, 181
Taunton Dene 23
Taylor, Barry 137
Taylor, G.W. 74
Tear Drop Inn, Wallingford 40
Tetsworth 141
Thame 23, 46, 66, 79, 125, 139, 148

Thame Park 66
Thames, River 23, 24, 30, 35,
    38, 40, 52, 65, 77, 98, 99,
    108, 113, 123, 146, 150,
    155, 165, 184, 187, 188
Theale 23
Thompson, Flora 6, 7, 74, 90,
    164, 180, 184
Thor Stone, Taston 13
Tip Cat 90
Tobias the Monk 33
Tom Tit's Song Book 159
Tongue, Ruth 140, 184
Tooker, Thomas 170
Top Oxon 6, 20, 182
Toussaints Abbey 20
Towersey 40, 133, 148
Tracy family 154
Treacle Well 93
Trinity College 79, 170, 171,
    173, 174
Trinity Sunday 52, 115
Tristan 31
Troy Town maze 20, 21
True John and Greedy Jack
    140
Tuckers 75
Turkish Knight 133, 134, 136
Turner, Revd Noel 159
Turpin, Dick 42
Tuslin, Ann 142
Twelfth Night 104, 105, 123,
    170

Uffenbach, Conrad van 64, 183
Uffington 15, 16, 17, 18, 50,
    132, 134, 136, 181, 182
Uffington Castle 18
University College 167, 176,
    179, 181
University Parks 168
University of Oxford 6, 108,
    116, 170, 182, 184, 188
Upton Lovell 34

Vale of White Horse 7, 13, 15,
    55, 62, 72, 74, 85, 87, 123
Victoria, Queen 27, 76, 123,
    160
Victoria, Princess Royal 160
Victoria & Albert Museum 27
village tales 165, 166
Vintners City Livery Company
    98, 99
Virgil's Aeniad 39

Waine family 55

Wake, Sir Baldwin 152
wakes 86, 121, 122
Walker, Joanna 141
Wallingford 30, 33, 40, 150,
    157
Wallingford Castle 30
Wantage 26, 42, 79, 84, 114,
    115, 121, 133, 138
Warborough 22
Wardington 94
Warland, John 59
washing 101, 102
Washinton, Sip 131
Wassailing 123
Watchfield 154
Watercress Queen 73
Waterperry 68
Waterstock 63
Watlington 15, 22, 98, 141
Watson, Right Revd Richard 66
Watts, Anne 100
wax images 142
Wayland's Smithy 13, 14, 15,
    115, 140, 181
weather lore 18, 94, 95, 96, 98
weddings 12, 52, 58, 59, 60, 61,
    62, 74, 98, 103
Wells, George 129, 130
Wells, William 'Jinky' 129, 184
Wendlebury 55
Wesley, John 42
West Hendred 133, 153
West, Martin 172, 173
Westmorland 177
Weston-on-the-Green 79
Weston-super-Mare 23
Wheatley 20, 78, 84, 95, 114,
    131, 133, 181
Whispering Knights 8, 9, 10,
    139
Whit Hunt 115, 116
White Hart, Henley-on-
    Thames 151
White ladies 145
Whitsun 86, 93, 109, 113, 114,
    119, 122, 125, 132, 182
Whitsun Ales 109, 113, 114
White Horse Hill 6, 7, 13, 15,
    16, 17, 18, 20, 25, 55, 87,
    157, 181
Widdowes, Thomas 39
wife selling 61
Wigginton 148
William the Conqueror 28
Williams, Alfred 74, 77, 165,
    184
Williams, Mel 120

Wilcote 146, 153
Wilcote, Lord and Lady 146
Wild hunt 145, 146
Williamscot 47, 48, 100
will-o'-the-wisp 139
Wilmot, John, Lord Rochester
    40
Winchcombe, Benedict 145
Winchester, Bishop of 171
Wisdom, Simon 61
witches 9, 11, 12, 15, 19, 78,
    80, 99, 101, 122, 140, 141,
    142, 144, 148,
Wise, Francis 14, 16, 17
Witney Feast 121
Witney 54, 55, 61, 74, 81, 88,
    102, 107, 115, 116, 121,
    122, 136, 138, 158
Witney blankets 74, 75
Wittenham 94, 133, 188
Wittenham Clumps 22
Wodhams, J.R. 68
Wood, Anthony 64, 93, 170,
    181
Wood, Miss 51
Wood, Mrs 51
Woodcote 146
Woodperry 79
Woodstock 11, 12, 30, 31, 39,
    43, 48, 62, 85, 114, 119,
    120, 132, 147, 158, 167,
    180, 185
Woodstock Manor 30, 31, 39,
    119
Woodstock Whitsun Ale 114
Wootton 99, 103, 119, 183
Worcester, Battle of 39, 40,
    42, 41
Worsham Lane 53
Wren, Sir Christopher 173
wrestling 18, 85, 87, 122
Wykeham, Sophia, Lady
    Wenman 66
Wykeham, William of 108
Wynkin de Worde 178
Wychwood 93, 108, 115, 125,
    132, 137, 140, 142, 158,
    159, 181, 182, 185, 189
Wythan 165

Yarnton 38, 54, 68, 69, 97, 153
Yarnton lot meadows 69
Yelford 158
Young, Mrs J. 51
Young, Will 46
York 42, 158, 154
Yorkshire 20, 70, 135